instru
handbook

Written by James Stevens and Penny Haire

www.rya.org.uk

Royal Yachting Association
RYA House, Ensign Way, Hamble, Southampton SO31 4YA
Tel: 0845 345 0400 Fax: 0845 345 0329
email: training@rya.org.uk website: www.rya.org.uk

All rights reserved. No part of this publication may be transmitted, stored in a retrieval system,
or transmitted, in any form or by any means, electronic, mechanical, photocopying, recording or
otherwise, without the prior permission of the publisher.
© Royal Yachting Association 1990
Revised edition 2004
Reprinted August 2008

Throughout this book the pronouns 'he', 'him' and 'his' have been used inclusively and are
intended to apply to both men and women. It is important in sport as elsewhere that women
and men should have equal status and equal opportunities.

CONTENTS

Side lines indicate changes from the previous edition.

INTRODUCTION

Participants in the RYA Cruising scheme range from young trainees on Tall Ships, skippers learning the intricacies of sailing a 26 foot bilge keeler in shoal water to a new owner learnng to berth a motorboat. Instructors must have a multitude of skills which have to be adapted to the type of vessel, the type of crew, or the pupil in the classroom. It is impractical to lay down specific techniques or devise an 'RYA method' in the same way as the RYA dinghy scheme. There are, of course, regulations concerning the equipment on board and the qualifications of instructors but in general this book lays down guidelines rather than rules. It is intended as a handbook for the new instructor and a reminder for the more experienced, of the standards required.

Much of the material has been gained from practical instructor updates, conferences, shorebased workshops and talking to the students on the receiving end of the scheme. The courses are continually under review as methods of sailing, navigation and instruction change.

COMMUNICATION WITH CENTRES AND INSTRUCTORS

Circulars are sent to both shorebased and practical centres two or three times a year to keep them informed of developments and changes in course syllabi, RYA policy etc. Regular information is also sent out by email and is available on the RYA website.

Separate conferences are held each year for shorebased and practical instructors. These allow for updating by the RYA, feedback from the instructors and a general forum for exchange of ideas. It is strongly recommended that all instructors should attend a conference every year.

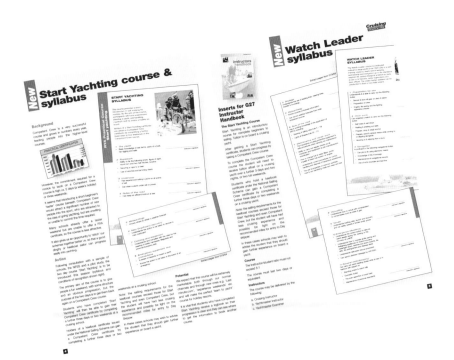

PRACTICAL SCHEME

RECOGNITION OF PRACTICAL CENTRES

Only recognised centres can issue certificates. Before a practical centre is recognised it must fulfil the following requirements:

Principal or Chief Instructor

There must be a Principal or Chief Instructor who holds an RYA Yachtmaster Certificate with a current instructor's endorsement (Power or Sail as appropriate). In large multi-discipline centres the Principal may appoint a Chief Instructor with responsibility for maintaining RYA standards. In these centres the Chief Instructor must hold a current Yachtmaster Instructor endorsement.

Vessel

A centre must have a sailing or motor cruising vessel available for inspection. Yachts used for instruction must conform with the Department of Transport Code of Practice for Small Commercial Vessels for Sail or Power as appropriate.

Briefly, to become certificated a stability category must be issued to the yacht determining its area of operation. Following a survey, a Small Commercial Vessels certificate can be issued by the RYA (or another certifying authority).

Yachts certificated under the older Sail Training Ship Code of Practice may also be used.

Details of the certification procedure can be found in the publication *The Safety of Small Commercial Sailing Vessels a Code of Practice*, and *The Safety of Small Commercial Motor Vessels a Code of Practice*, both available from HMSO or the RYA.

Administration

The centre must comply with certain administrative requirements such as carrying a safety policy.

Centres should ensure that administration is conducted efficiently.

Recognition is normally only granted to *bona fide* cruising centres offering a full programme of courses.

Recognition will normally be refused to a centre applying under a name that is the same or similar to an existing Recognised Training Centre (RTC).

Recognised practical centres pay an annual fee and are subject to annual and spot check inspections. During inspections the standard of instruction and condition of the boats is checked.

The Principal or Chief Instructor is responsible for ensuring that the correct RYA standards are maintained, these include the conduct and standards of the instructors as well as yacht equipment and maintenance.

Every effort should be made by the Principal / Chief Instructor to resolve any complaints as quickly as possible. Receipt by the RYA of an unreasonable number of substantiated complaints against a centre may result in suspension / withdrawal of the centre's recognition.

Practical centres can purchase from the RYA, practical course completion certificates and other RYA publications, which are listed on the Account Holders price list for practical cruising centres.

The Principal must ensure that the centre and its instructors are adequately insured.

Recognition is automatically revoked upon the Principal's death or retirement, cessation of active instruction or sale of the establishment. Recognition can also be withdrawn at the discretion of the RYA.

Where a centre has more than one operating base, a Chief Instructor who holds at least a RYA Yachtmaster Certificate with a current Instructor endorsement (power or sail as appropriate) must be appointed to supervise each location

The Principal / Proprietor of the parent centre must take overall responsibility for the centre's activities at all bases.

Withdrawal of recognition or instructor qualification

The RYA Training Committee can withdraw recognition for contravention of the rules or spirit of recognition.

The RYA may, at its discretion, refuse or withdraw recognition if, in its reasonable opinion, it does not have confidence in the training centres management or ability to uphold RYA standards.

The Training Committee can also withdraw Instructor qualifications where due cause is shown.

A centre or individual wishing to appeal against the decision of the Training Committee may bring their case to an RYA tribunal that will be convened for the purpose.

Advertising

Recognised centres may use the RYA logo, details of which are available from the RYA.

Centres must ensure they do not use the name of the RYA to advertise any activities (such as boat sales) not covered by the terms of recognition.

Centres must ensure that any advertising material relating to RYA activities complies with the British Codes of Advertising and Sales Promotion.

QUALIFICATION OF PRACTICAL INSTRUCTORS

Principals of sailing centres

The Principal or Chief Instructor of a sailing centre shall hold a current Yachtmaster Instructor qualification for sail and/or power as appropriate.

Sail and power

All Instructors teaching RYA practical courses must hold a Yachtmaster Offshore Certificate of Competence. Additionally all instructors must hold either a Cruising Instructor, Yachtmaster Instructor or Yachtmaster Examiner Qualification.

Yachtmaster Instructor qualifying courses

Eligibility:

64 years maximum age limit	Commercial Endorsement
YM Offshore Certificate of Competence	• Basic Sea Survival
• VHF (Restricted) Operators Licence	• Medical Fitness Examination (ML5 or ENG1) or medical issued by a National Maritime Authority
• First Aid Certificate	

During the course each candidate's skippering ability is tested, particularly the skills of pilotage, boat handling and navigation. The candidate should be able to demonstrate any part of the Coastal Skipper syllabus in G15 or G18 and to explain any part of the Coastal Skipper/Yachtmaster Offshore shorebased course.

The candidates will be taught how to conduct RYA courses and be shown some of the recommended techniques and some of the pitfalls to be avoided. The five days will be similar in many ways to a normal training course with skippered passages, sessions on boat handling and navigation followed by debriefings. The emphasis is on how to instruct rather than how to skipper or crew a yacht.

Teaching potential is also assessed. Essentially this means being able to generate interest and communicate clearly on deck and at the chart table. The best instructors are first class sailors who can run cheerful, well organised and instructional cruises.

Most problems and complaints from students on courses stem from inconsiderate and unsympathetic behaviour by the instructor. Living with different groups of strangers at close quarters calls for considerable reserves of fortitude and sociability. Potential instructors who are likely to upset their crews may be failed.

At the end of the course each candidate is fully debriefed, given the reasons for pass or failure and an appraisal of strengths and weaknesses. This is intended to be a positive and constructive method of helping instructors to be self critical.

Sail
Qualifying courses are normally of five days duration and are run by the RYA and the National Centres at Plas Menai and Cumbrae.

Power
Qualifying courses are normally of three days duration and are organised in the same way as sailing courses.

Updating
Both sail and power instructors must attend a two day updating course at least every five years to retain their qualification. If issued, the Instructor endorsement can be valid for 5 years, at the RYA's discretion. Then retirement age for Instructors is 70.

Probationary courses
Instructors who have passed qualifying courses may run all RYA practical courses and apply for recognition as Principal of a recognised centre. Before the endorsement is awarded they must satisfactorily complete two RYA practical courses at a recognised centre within 12 months of the qualifying course. A newly qualified instructor who is Principal of a centre may sign for his own courses. Failure to complete two courses within 12 months may result in withdrawal of the qualification.

The purpose of this requirement is to ensure that the instructor's endorsement is awarded only to those who intend to use the qualification.

Cruising Instructor qualification
Valid for Instructors teaching Competent Crew/Helmsmans and Day Skipper practical courses.

Eligibility:

64 years maximum age limit	Commercial Endorsement
YM Offshore Certificate of Competence	• Basic Sea Survival
• VHF (Restricted) Operators Licence	• Medical Fitness Examination
• First Aid Certificate	(ML5 or ENG1) or medical issued
	by a National Maritime Authority

Validity
The qualification is valid for five years. After 5 years the RYA Cruising Instructor must either be re-tested, or preferably take a Yachtmaster Instructor Qualifying Course.

Assessment

The assessment must be conducted by the Centre Principal or Chief Instructor. No more than two candidates may be examined in one day. Candidates will be assessed on their general suitability for instruction as well as specific skills.

Syllabus

Instructional Technique

Can:

- Set up tasks and teaching sessions appropriate to individual students.
- Brief clearly to all the crew or individuals.
- Ensure tasks are undertaken correctly and safely.
- Debrief and provide plan for improvement.
- Give convincing practical demonstrations of any part of the Competent Crew or Helmsman   course and Day Skipper Practical course, including the following:

    Knots; sail handling and trim; man overboard; mooring; pilotage by day and night; IRPCS; basic meteorology; navigation to Day Skipper Practical standard; skippering ability including comprehensive knowledge of the yacht and its equipment.

- Explain clearly any part of the Competent Crew or Helmsman and Day Skipper Shorebased courses.

Knowledge

RYA Competent Crew or Helmsman and Day Skipper Shorebased and Practical courses. *Understands:*

- RYA Scheme
- Levels of competence required for award of certificates
- Duty of care
- Environmental protection issues
- Policies and procedures specific to the centre

Safety

Has a personal standard and style of skippering which engenders confidence in beginners. Can give a comprehensive safety briefing using the centre's instructions. *Understands:*

- Centre's safety policy
- Accident reporting procedure
- Care of yacht

Personal Skills

Has the ability to welcome strangers on board and run a relaxed, happy ship. *Understands:*

- How to gain feedback and deal with difficult customers and complaints
- The need for high personal standards

Instructors teaching Coastal Skipper courses must have a current instructor or examiner endorsement.

Commercial endorsement

Instructors working on commercial vessels certificated under the Code of Practice must have a commercial endorsement to their Ocean or Offshore Yachtmasters certificate.

To obtain a commercial endorsement send the following to the RYA:

1. Copy of Sea Survival Certificate (issued following a one day course).*
2. Report of a medical fitness examination (form available from the RYA).*
3. Original Yachtmaster or Coastal Skipper certificate (i.e. not photocopy).
4. £17 fee

* Or outside the UK, the Nationally approved equivalent.

First aid

Instructors must hold one of the following:

RYA one day Small Craft First Aid Course

Ships Captains Medical Course

First Aid at Sea

First Aid at Work (St John's, Red Cross or St Andrew's)

Public First Aid (SJA,SAA)

Medical or nursing qualification of equivalent or higher standard.

Overseas: A First Aid Certificate issued by a National Authority.

The first aid and commercial endorsement requirements apply to Yachtmasters, Cruising Instructors and Yachtmaster Instructors.

CONDUCT OF PRACTICAL COURSES

Centres must issue RYA certificates as soon as possible on completion of RYA courses.

Sailing courses

The pupil instructor ratio must not exceed 5:1. Any customers on board for other reasons (e.g.to gain experience or mileage) are included in this ratio.

Start Yachting courses must be run over two days or equivalent, or one weekend.

Competent crew courses may be run over five consecutive days, three weekends or a two and three day weekend.

Day Skipper courses must be run over 5 consecutive days or three weekends.

Coastal Skipper courses must be run over 5 consecutive days.

All courses, with the exception of Start Yachting should last a minimum of 116 hours.

It is unacceptable for a boat to day sail from her home port throughout the course. The instructor should plan an itinerary, taking into account the ability of the crew, the weather conditions and the requirements to cover the syllabus in an interesting, varied and informative way.

The instructor should sleep on board for a minimum of four nights.

During the course the yacht should sail a minimum of 100 miles.

Each member of the crew should experience at least four hours of night watchkeeping.

Day Skipper and Coastal Skipper courses should be conducted on yachts under 15m.

Motor cruising courses

The pupil instructor ratio must not exceed 5:1.

The Helmsman's course shall last a minimum of two days.

Day Skipper courses shall be at least four days.

Coastal Skipper courses shall last five days.

If the Helmsman's course and Day Skipper course are combined the duration of the combined course may be five days.

The Helmsman's course may be non-residential, but if so, evening theory sessions will be required to cover the syllabus.

Day Skipper and Coastal Skipper courses should cover a minimum of 100 miles and each member of the crew should experience at least four hours of night watch keeping.

Day Skipper courses may be non-residential but evening sessions are required each day in order to fulfil the syllabus adequately.

Coastal Skipper courses shall be residential.

Courses in non-tidal waters

Competent Crew and Helmsmans courses may be run in non-tidal waters. For the purposes of centres operating in Gibraltar, Tidal Day Skipper and Coastal Skipper courses must be run West of a line joining Gibraltar to Ceuta. In the Baltic, Tidal Day Skipper and Coastal Skipper courses must be run West of a line joining the Skaw to Kristiansand. Non-tidal courses may of course be run in the Mediterranean and Baltic.

Own boat tuition

Practical centres may offer instruction for RYA certificates in a student's boat. Before doing so however, the principal must ensure that the boat is in sound condition and is adequately equipped both for safety and for effective instruction.

There is no requirement for a Small Commercial Vessel Certificate for a boat which is being used for the owner's instruction and that of his or her family or friends.

A centre may not offer only own boat instruction.

Swimmers

It is strongly recommended that all those participating in the sport of cruising should be able to swim. It is essential that the instructor in charge of a course should know if any members of the course are non-swimmers and should require non-swimmers to wear life jackets at all times when on deck or in a dinghy.

Duty of care

Instructors must always remember that they are sailing with relatively inexperienced people, who may not be able to make a sound assessment of the risks inherent in sailing. Instructors should not hesitate to require safety harnesses or lifejackets to be worn by crew members when the circumstances make it prudent for them to do so.

Alcohol consumption

While on duty ashore and afloat practical instructors are required by law to keep their alcohol consumption below the maximum permitted for driving road vehicles.

Health Declaration

All RYA recognised teaching centress are strongly recommended to include a health declaration in their booking forms. Such information must be passed on by the Principal to the individual instructor responsible for the student. One possible format for the declaration is given below:

Details of any medical treatment being received (if none write none)

I declare that to the best of my knowledge, I am not suffering from epilepsy, disability, giddy spells, asthma, diabetes, angina, or other heart condition, and I am fit to participate in the course.

Signature -- Date ---------------------------------

The information sent out to students should stress that illnesses or medical conditions need not necessarily prevent the student from taking a full part in the course, but the Principal or instructor must be aware of any potential problem. If a student is in any doubt about his fitness to take part in a practical course, his GP should be able to advise.

OVERSEAS CENTRES

RYA requirements for practical sailing centres operating yachts outside the United Kingdom

1. Temporary detachment of a yacht from a UK-based sailing centre .

   A UK sailing centre may run RYA courses abroad as long as the following conditions are met:

   1.1 The yacht is available for inspection in the UK for at least six months each year.

   1.2 When the yacht is operating overseas she is under the direct control of a Yachtmaster Instructor.

   1.3 Except for passages to and from the UK and the occasional long cruise, crew turnarounds shall be at the same base port where the instructor can be contacted. The RYA shall be informed of this address.

   1.4 The Principal of the centre shall be responsible for the standards of tuition and yacht maintenance.

   1.5 Sailing yachts must have a Small Commercial Vessel Certificate.

2. Practical cruising centres permanently based outside the United Kingdom must apply for overseas recognition. The following conditions must be met:

   2.1 The primary language of instruction is English.

   2.2 All students will be provided with course feedback reports as and when required by the RYA.

   2.3 Shall have a permanent address abroad.

   2.4 Shall pay overseas recognition fees, which will be set at a rate to cover the cost of an inspection.

   2.5 Crew turnarounds to be at the overseas base port except for the occasional long cruise.

   2.6 No 'satellite' centres in other ports. If a centre wishes to base a yacht at another port, separate recognition must be obtained.

   2.7 All other requirements for UK yachts apply, including the requirement to conform with the Code of Practice. Foreign flagged yachts certificated for commercial use in their own country must still carry the equipment for compliance with Department of Transport Code of Practice, or ISAF special regulations category 2 or 3, as appropriate. Foreign flagged yachts however cannot carry a Small Commercial Vessel Certificate.

THE ORGANISATION AND CONDUCT OF COASTAL SKIPPER AND YACHTMASTER OFFSHORE EXAMS

INTRODUCTION

The purpose of these notes is to set guidelines for the conduct of exams.

AUTHORISATION OF EXAMS

All exams must be authorised by an examination centre or booked online at www.rya.org.uk.

Overseas exams must be organised through an RYA Training Centre recognised for practical cruising courses. The centre must notify the RYA of any overseas exams and the location must be approved by the RYA.

An individual candidate who applies to a centre may be put in touch with an examiner to make the detailed arrangements for the exam.

Examination centres may give standing authorisation to sailing centres which have a programme of exams, to contact examiners direct. Centres must receive notification of every exam carried out and must ensure that a standing authorisation is not used as a means of examiner selection by any sailing centre. A centre which has a standing authorisation must use a number of different examiners and should only use examiners on its own staff in exceptional circumstances if no other examiner is available.

PAYMENT OF EXAM FEE

The exam fee is payable by the candidate to the RYA. Examiners must ensure that the exam report is accompanied by the appropriate cheque. Examiners may not accept any payment from candidates for expenses incurred in connection with an exam.

CANDIDATE'S ELIGIBILITY TO TAKE AN EXAM

Before the start of an exam the examiner must verify the candidate's claim to have the specified sea experience.

All candidates must complete and sign the exam application form, which includes a statement of qualifying experience.

If there is any doubt as to whether or not the necessary seatime has been completed the examiner should point this out to the candidate and give him the opportunity to withdraw his application.

Candidates for Coastal Skipper and Yachtmaster Offshore must hold a radio operator's certificate. In most cases this will be the Restricted (VHF only) Certificate of Competence in Radiotelephony but any higher qualification, such as the Restricted or General Certificate of Competence or, for foreign nationals an equivalent certificate issued by their own administration, is acceptable.

Candidates for Yachtmaster Offshore must hold a current first aid certificate. Most certificates issued by St.John's, Red Cross, St. Andrew's are acceptable. Note that for commercial use, only certificates listed on page 3 are acceptable. For foreign nationals, an equivalent certificate issued by a national body is acceptable.

GENERAL STANDARDS TO BE SET BY EXAMINERS

It is important that examiners are above criticism in their general conduct in all their dealings with candidates. In particular, examiners must:

Be punctual in keeping appointments for exams.

Set a standard of dress and appearance which is at least as high as that of the candidate.

Respect the candidate's or boat owner's wishes on smoking below decks while on board.

Be courteous to candidates and crew throughout the exam.

These are, of course, points of which all examiners will be aware. The reason for including this reminder is that a candidate who fails is liable to look for points on which to attack the examiner and the system, so it is important not to provide any ammunition.

CONTENT OF EXAMINATION

General

The content of the exam is set by the syllabus in the RYA publication G15 and the headings in the report form.

There are two general principles which should be taken as an overall guide.

1. It is the examiner's task to give the candidate the opportunity to show that he is a competent skipper.
2. At the end of the exam the candidate should feel, whatever the outcome, that he has had a full, fair, and searching test.

CANDIDATE NUMBERS AND DURATION OF EXAM

Practical exams

For planning purposes, the following times should be used as guidelines:

Coastal Skipper:	One candidate	6-10 hours
	More than one candidate	4-8 hours per candidate
Yachtmaster Offshore:	One candidate	8-12 hours
	More than one candidate	5-9 hours per candidate

All exams should, whenever possible, include time underway in darkness. It is, however, accepted that this will not be possible in high latitudes in mid-summer.

Examiners should not plan to examine more than two candidates in any 24 hour period. If everything goes well, it may be possible to examine three candidates in 24 hours but this will not always be the case. If the weather conditions are unhelpful or candidates turn out to be borderline cases it will be impossible to do justice to more than two candidates in 24 hours. It is also important that examiners should take a realistic view of their own concentration span and should not attempt prolonged exam sessions. No more than four candidates should be examined during any one session, or the process becomes repetitive and predictable.

CONVERSION PRACTICAL EXAMINATIONS

Holders of the Yachtmaster Offshore Sail Certificate may take a conversion examination to obtain the Yachtmaster Offshore Power Certificate.

Experience

At least half the required experience for Yachtmaster must be in a power vessel such as a motor cruiser i.e:

1250 miles

25 days

3 days as skipper

3 passages over 60 miles including

1 overnight and

1 as skipper

The exam will take about three hours. The Examiner may ask questions or set tasks on any part of the syllabus but will concentrate on those sections which are markedly different in a motor cruiser e.g. boat handling, passage planning, radar.

Yachtmaster Offshore power candidates may convert to sail. The same rules apply but the exam may be slightly longer.

The exam fee set by the RYA is approximately half that of a full examination.

EXERCISE SCENARIOS

In order to carry out a thorough test, examiners may find it convenient to devise exercise scenarios. This may sometimes be a valid and acceptable method but there are a number of pitfalls which must be avoided.

It is important that the examiner is careful to give a full explanation of the scenario, which must be as simple as possible and credible to the candidate. If the examiner fails to do this, the exam degenerates into a role-playing farce.

The scenario must be designed to test a particular skill and the examiner must confine his assessment to the candidate's demonstration of that skill. A candidate will seldom accept failure if the reason is inability to complete an artificial exercise to the examiner's satisfaction. The reason for failure must be expressed in terms of failure to demonstrate a particular skill.

STRESS MANAGEMENT

The candidate's ability to make sound decisions under pressure is an integral part of the test. The examiner must ensure that the pressure is from the specific circumstances of the situation and not from the examiner personally.

Candidates react to the exam situation in a variety of different ways and the examiner must make an early assessment of the extent to which exam nerves are going to be a barrier to a fair test. The examiner should, by his personal demeanour, put the candidate at his ease and make sure that at no time does the test degenerate into a personality confrontation.

The examiner can unwittingly build up stress in a number of ways. He should be particularly careful to avoid, for instance:

Any remark which the candidate might interpret as being gratuitously disparaging.

Apparent secretiveness about his intentions during the exam.

Prolonged periods of silence.

Quick fire questions.

Irrelevant questions when the candidate is trying hard to concentrate on the task in hand.

Stress can be reduced by:

1. Setting a straightforward practical task and giving a genuine 'well done' at the end (assuming it was successful).
2. Taking an interest in the candidate and communicating in a non confrontational way.
3. A sense of humour – but do not make the candidate the butt of the joke, and do avoid sarcasm.

USE OF CREW

It is important to make it clear to the candidate and his crew what role the crew is expected to play. Everyone on board must be made aware that the examiner has to test the candidate and any attempt by the crew to prompt the skipper is liable to lose rather than gain points for the candidate. This does not mean that the crew should act dumb, they should play a full part in sailing the boat but they must not anticipate the candidate's decisions. The most important part of the exam is the candidate's ability to lead, motivate and communicate with the crew so the examiner must be careful not to erect artificial barriers between skipper and crew.

SPECIFIC ASPECTS OF PRACTICAL EXAMS

The exam must be set in the context that the candidate is the skipper of the boat. It is important to make it clear that the examiner is there only to observe and report. The candidate is the skipper at all times with full responsibility for the safety of the boat and crew. The examiner should exercise control over the boat only so far as it is necessary to set up a test and should not take direct control unless he feels that it is necessary to prevent damage to crew or boat.

Preparation of boat and crew

The aim of this section is to test whether the candidate knows what checks on boat and equipment should be carried out and what points should be included in a briefing to a newly-joined crew.

Passage planning

The test should show that the candidate understands the passage-planning process. The test may be pre-set so that the candidate arrives for the exam with a passage already planned.

Boat handling (entering and leaving harbour)

The test should, so far as possible, be so arranged that if the candidate is going to get it wrong he can be allowed to do so without causing damage. This avoids any subsequent question as to whether a 'failure' was that of the examiner's nerve rather than the candidate's ability.

Pilotage

Whenever possible the candidate should be required to take the boat into confined waters with which he is unfamiliar.

Boat handling (open water)

The test should require the candidate to sail the boat efficiently. This is an area which calls for fine judgement on the part of the examiner, who must distinguish between the ability to set the boat up to win races and the ability to use the sails with an acceptable degree of efficiency.

Man overboard recovery

Every candidate should be required to carry out a man overboard recovery exercise. Ensure that the candidate is clear whether the engine can be used.

Navigation and chartwork

In general the candidate should be encouraged to navigate as he would normally. If he chooses to do no formal chartwork and rely instead on 'by-eye' navigation, the examiner must decide whether or not this is safe.

Chartwork must be tested and in order to do so the examiner may have to impose a scenario which makes chartwork essential for the safe navigation of the boat.

Navigation with and without access to electronic position fixing systems should be included.

Deckwork and general seamanship

There are two aspects to be tested; decision making and practical ability to implement decisions. Do not assume that because a candidate regards himself as a skipper he can carry out elementary routine tasks. Occasionally you will encounter a candidate who cannot tie a bowline.

IRPCS

The test should show that the candidate knows the correct lights/shapes for his own boat, can recognise any vessel by special lights or shapes, assess risk of collision and take the correct action in any situation where risk of collision exists. Questions requiring retained knowledge of specific local regulations should not be used.

Meteorology

The test should include knowledge of what forecasts are available, the interpretation of forecasts and visible phenomena. This section of the exam should be related to passage planning and strategy, it should not be an academic exercise.

Overall ability as skipper

All items should be tested within the overall context of the candidate's ability as skipper.

The level of difficulty of the test and the standard of expertise required to pass depends on whether the exam is for Coastal Skipper or Yachtmaster Offshore. At Coastal Skipper level the situations should be simple and the candidate should be allowed as much time as he needs to complete each test. Crew management should only be that necessary for short passages. At Yachtmaster Offshore level the test situations may be complex and may be set with pressure to complete the situation quickly. The candidate is expected to be able to organise and manage a crew on passages of up to 48 hours.

Check lists

A check list of items to be tested during the exam is set out in Appendix 3. There will never be time to cover everything on the list and the purpose is to help to plan a well balanced exam.

Weather limitations

If there is insufficient wind to make a fair assessment of the candidate's sailing ability the examiner and candidate should arrange a mutually convenient date for a re-test. There is no additional fee payable by the candidate or to the examiner.

Adverse weather (strong winds or poor visibility) are an integral part of the exam process. It is reasonable for the examiner to fail a candidate who declines to go to sea in conditions under which a candidate capable of passing the exam could safely put to sea. There will be occasions on which it is unsafe to carry out a test, in which case it will be necessary to arrange another date for the exam.

Pass/fail recommendation

In deciding whether or not a candidate should pass or fail, a broad view of overall performance should be taken. No candidate is perfect and the examiner must therefore balance strengths and weaknesses when coming to a pass/fail decision. In making this decision the examiner must heavily mark down any indication of unsafe practice, lack of knowledge or poor application of IRPCS.

Post exam de-brief

At the end of every exam the examiner should carry out a de-briefing session with the candidate. The examiner should stress that he is stating his personal view of how the exam went and that the final pass/fail decision rests with the Yachtmaster Qualification Panel (although in practice it is most unusual for an examiner's recommendation to be reversed).

If the candidate is being recommended for a certificate the de-brief can be quite short and take the form of 'Well done,.....'

but

If the candidate is not to be recommended, the purpose of the de-brief is to make the process of failure as kind and as positive as possible. Praise any good points which emerged during the test but do not gloss over the bad points, which should be treated in the vein..' What you might do to improve this so that you pass next time is......'

EXAM REPORTS

The exam report must be completed and forwarded to the RYA at the earliest possible opportunity. Centres may also require notification that an exam has been carried out.

The exam report is in two sections: a factual report on the candidate's ability and (for failures) a recommendation on how to remedy any deficiencies.

Most of those who fail are sent a copy of the exam report so it is important that the de-brief and exam report are not contradictory. An exception to this general rule is made in the case of disastrously bad candidates, who are sent a conciliatory letter. To send them the report would be rubbing salt into the wound.

PARTIAL RE-EXAMINATION

A candidate who fails in a single section of the exam and is good in all other sections may be re-tested by the same examiner, within a period of six weeks. In such cases an additional fee, as laid down by the RYA, is to be charged. The re-test procedure is intended primarily for candidates who fail one of the 'memory test' subjects but examiners may use their discretion in asking candidates to take a re-test in any subject. The exam report should not be forwarded until the re-examination has been completed.

BARRIERS TO EXAMINATION

An examiner should not examine a candidate who is a personal friend, who he has taught or who he has previously failed in an examination.

Examiners must examine only in boats of a type of which they have experience and which they would themselves be confident to skipper.

INTERNATIONAL CERTIFICATE OF COMPETENCE

The ICC is required by some European countries for certain categories of pleasure boat. RYA publications C1 and C2 *Planning a Foreign Cruise* give the details of the certification required for all European countries.

Yachtsmen can obtain an ICC from the RYA by completing an application form and either:

1. Sending a copy of a practical certificate at Day Skipper level or above.
2. Re-applying on expiry of a Helmsman's Overseas Certificate of Competence (predecessor to the ICC)
3. Or passing a practical and oral test at a test centre.

The issue of the ICC is free to RYA members. Non-members are charged a fee.

TEST CENTRES

Only RYA recognised practical centres or affiliated clubs with qualified testers may be used as test centres. Centres and clubs may only offer tests for the disciplines for which their testers are qualified.

TESTERS

Testers can be Yachtmaster instructors or Yachtmasters who have attended a tester training course.

Conduct of tests

The syllabus and tasks required for the practical test are given on the application form available from the RYA.

Oral　　　　The RYA can provide test centres with sample questions.

Practical　　The purpose of the practical test is to give every candidate the opportunity to show that they are capable of skippering a boat without endangering or damaging other people, boats or the marine environment.

Some coaching is permitted during the test to help the candidate achieve the required standard.

The candidate can reasonably expect politeness and good humour from the person carrying out the test.

The biggest barrier to a successful test is the candidate's nerves. This can be overcome by the following:

a. Having a friendly and relaxed manner yourself.

b. Getting the candidate involved in an activity as quickly as possible (without putting pressure on them).

c. If the candidate has carried out a manoeuvre well, then say so.

d. Don't be inscrutable, talk to the candidate and the rest of the crew.

The existence of any test implies that there must be people who will not be up to standard. The tester's most difficult job is to break the bad news as gently as possible.

This can be made easier by:

a. Making sure the candidate knows that his overall performance has been below standard. In many cases it will be obvious because of the failure to complete an exercise. Try to set practical tests which can be failed without requiring the tester to stop the exercise or take over control.

b. De-brief constructively. Praise what was done well. Suggest ways of improving what was done badly rather than simply stating that it was below an acceptable standard.

c. If possible, organise a re-test of the tasks which were not achieved. A deferment is always more palatable than a straight fail.

INSTRUCTIONAL TECHNIQUE

Sailing instruction is essentially a process of brief, task, debrief. The students are there to handle the equipment and to actually do the tasks.

No one teaches how to tie a bowline by simply talking about it. Even a demonstration of tying a bowline only takes you a little further forward. Until the student actually has the rope in his hand, he is learning very little.

On a sailing course, you should start sailing and involving the students in practical tasks as soon as possible. A safety brief is required but don't spend time talking about the theory of sailing or how to tack - get out and do it. Once people start to see the boat and equipment being used, or better still, doing it themselves, they will pick up the concept fairly quickly.

BRIEFING

You must be able to explain what is required clearly – a difficult problem on a lively yacht on a windy day. If only half the crew are listening, calm the situation by heaving to, and sit in the cockpit. If you are giving a demonstration draw their attention to the part of the boat that is important at the time. For example, when demonstrating a mooring pick up under sail, point out wind direction indicator, the position of the mainsheet, the sideways effect of the tide, etc. This will ensure that you hold their attention and they are not distracted by the other yachts, ferries etc. while you are talking. As far as possible position yourself and the crew so that they can see you – talking to the backs of heads is a common and basic mistake. Make your briefs exactly that – brief, the anecdotes can come later.

The task

Students practising pilotage, boat handling, or any skill on board must be given the opportunity to feel they are responsible for that task. Do not continually interrupt, if you have briefed well it should not be necessary. If events start going wrong, a quiet   word will allow the student to correct the error and redirect the crew if necessary. Never elbow students out of the way to demonstrate your skill, the idea is that they demonstrate theirs.

You must not, of course, allow the yacht to stand into danger. The point at which you step in depends on the situation but also on the level of the student's ability. Allowing mistakes to be made is often a useful way of making a point. For example, if the tide is flooding and the bottom soft, running aground might be a useful exercise particularly for skippers who have never had the experience. Always ask yourself 'Is this error a useful teaching opportunity?' not 'It'll serve him right if we pile aground'.

DEBRIEFING

Debriefing is one of the most important skills of a sailing instructor. Done well it is informative, positive, good natured and helpful: done badly, it can be destructive and demoralising.

At the end of a debrief students should be clear about what happened, their strengths and weaknesses and be fired with enthusiasm to try again and improve. They should never lose their self esteem or motivation.

Debrief as soon as possible after a task. Don't be tempted at the end of a night passage to debrief next morning, you will be surprised at how keen the skipper is to discuss the trip. Similarly, as navigation, pilotage or seamanship situations arise, debrief succinctly – underway if you can. Sometimes, particularly beating to windward, the crew and perhaps you, are not up to meaningful discussions about yachting and would prefer waiting until harbour.

You must observe each task very carefully. For this reason it is best not to take too active a part in crewing the yacht. Often a problem develops quite a lot earlier than is perceived by the skipper. If necessary make notes, but do this unobtrusively, it is very threatening to stand at the backstay with a notebook. On the subject of backstays, it is a useful vantage point close to the controls but you should remember that it can be off-putting for the helmsman and it is a poor position from which to deliver a debrief.

If you have time, heave to or stop the boat. Take the student in question off the helm and sit in the cockpit or around the saloon table if possible. A good way of debriefing is to ask the student what happened or if they would act differently next time. They will usually react by saying what was wrong, giving you the opportunity of reminding them what went right and discussing how to improve. Above all listen to what is being said to you. Many instructors used to taking command and issuing instructions neglect the student's comments and are therefore unaware as to whether anything is getting across or not.

ADVERSE WEATHER

Gales

Sailing Instructors should never be caught out by gales. Sail training yachts have been screened for stability and can withstand a gale in calm water. In fact it is often a highlight of the week to sail along a weather shore in a gale. Opportunities for boat handling become less but as soon as the wind moderates a little the storm sails can be used safely and for practising manoeuvres without damage.

Fog

Thick fog is the only condition that can bring yachting to a standstill. Radiation (land) fog causes the worst visibility but fortunately this rarely lasts more than half a day.

Advection (sea) fog which often gives visibility of a few hundred metres can be regarded as an opportunity for contour navigation. The crew will be as enthusiastic as the instructor, while you remain positive so will they.

Calm

This is the hardest condition in which to run a course. Your best action is to keep close to the land, practice boat handling and be more ambitious than usual with the pilotage exercises. Avoid long passages under power and avoid scenario games except perhaps blind pilotage. On spring tides you might be able to use the tide induced wind and on the flood tide you should be able to explore creeks and inlets further than usual.

KEEPING STUDENTS INFORMED

RYA certificates provide a great incentive to book courses. Unfortunately, because a measure of competence is involved, they can become a discouragement to the weak student who feels a failure as the prospect of a certificate fades.

It is essential that the instructor keeps everyone informed as to their progress. Talk to each student (preferably individually) early in the course and be honest about where they stand now and what they can hope to achieve. This could involve breaking the news that a Coastal Skipper certificate might not be possible by the end of the week. Temper this by explaining how much can be achieved and agree between you to get the best possible value out of the course. From then on you are acting as a coach, indicating strengths and weaknesses and giving encouragement. Point out how much has been achieved as the week progresses so that at the final debrief you can both be satisfied that the course was worthwhile.

If you fail to keep students informed, tension will build up on board with students discussing in whispers whether they are passing or failing and during the final debrief your teaching may be blamed for the lack of results. This lack of communication between instructor and student is one of the commonest reasons for complaint about RYA courses. Remember that many of the people you teach are highly successful and respected in their own field. The only skill you may have that they haven't is the ability to skipper a yacht and instruct sailing. You must ensure they retain their dignity and a positive attitude towards you and the sport. Do not underestimate this part of the job – it is one of the most skillful aspects of instructing. Really talented instructors receive letters of thanks from students who have not been awarded a certificate.

The vast majority of students enjoy being on board, understand the difficulties of yachting and make concessions to the vagaries of their instructor and their fellow humans. Unfortunately, a few do become prickly and complain. The root of this is often an overestimation of ability but it can be compounded by inconsiderate behaviour by the instructor. A student who does not drink will be unimpressed by a nautical pub crawl even if the tuition is good. Everyone on board must be seen to do their share of pleasant and unpleasant tasks and also receive equal amounts of tuition. Do not give a potential complainant ammunition.

However, the occasional student can be difficult and disrupt the course. Probably the best way of tackling this is to say to them privately... 'look I know that you don't mean to do this but the way you come over to the rest of the crew is rather abrasive when you skipper the yacht/not appearing to do your share of the washing up' etc. While this might not always go down too well it is your best chance of clearing the air. Sometimes nothing works and you have to make the best you can of the week. If you think a student might complain, talk to the Principal of the Centre as soon as possible. It is often useful to write an account of the course in case the RYA is asked to investigate.

A number of problems have been caused by instructors becoming short tempered and anti-social through lack of time off. Everyone is susceptible to this problem when running too many consecutive courses, and Centre Principals should monitor their instructors carefully for this deterioration.

PLANNING THE COURSE

Most centres are situated in areas of sheltered water where courses can continue in virtually any weather. However, the world does not end at the Needles and in order to give students experience of offshore yachting, you need to spend some time in the open sea. As with recreational cruising, it is a mistake to promise an itinerary at the beginning of the week. The weather and the students' requirements will determine what you do. For example, a group of good dinghy sailors who can handle the boat might benefit from a longer passage through shipping lanes. Good navigators who need boat handling and pilotage practice should stay closer to the land.

It is unprofessional to arrive for a course without having studied charts and tides in the area. Discuss with the Principal good places for teaching, and find out where the yacht is welcome and where it is not. Avoid being too ambitious, particularly on the first day: even on Coastal Skipper courses the first manoeuvres take longer than you expect. Involve the students as much as possible in the planning.

Your first course

Hardened confident instructors have all been anxious about their first course. Your best plan is to research the area and arrive early to become familiar with the yacht, if possible practice handling it before the students arrive. Make a list of the points you wish to make during the safety brief and at the beginning of each day make a note of the topics and tasks that you might cover.

When the students arrive welcome them aboard and ask them about themselves and their experience. Learn their names immediately. Organise the accommodation and explain what you hope to do during the week. Be honest about your experience and invite them to ask you about anything they do not understand. If you come across as a sincere yachtsman or woman who is doing your best the crew will be willing you to succeed even if your technique is unpolished. If you give them an over-inflated view of yourself you will lose their confidence.

If you make an error admit it, think clearly and put it right. No-one gives perfect demonstrations every time, but you should be able to stay in charge and correct a misjudgment. Make sure your navigation and knowledge of the theory is up to Yachtmaster standard. If you are rusty on this, purchase the past papers from the RYA and do some revision before the course. Remember your trainee skippers have probably just passed the shorebased course.

Being slightly nervous before your first course is a good quality, it shows that you care and want to make it a success. At the end, thinking of all the things you should have done during the week is also a good quality, it means you are evaluating and improving what you do.

The Principal of the Centre is there to give you help and advice – use it.

On the first day, having covered the safety brief (preferably the evening before), set off as soon as practicable. The first sail hoist will be slow and inelegant and so will the first tack, but the learning curve will be far quicker than on any pre-course theory. Even on an advanced course, deck work and some steering skills will have to be re-learnt. Each student will have to be taught individually to some extent; the instructor is acting as a coach rather than a class teacher. Put in a reef, change a headsail, keeping yourself free to help if necessary. Move the crew around and change back to the original sail plan. Before each task give a short brief or demonstration. Help during the manoeuvre, and afterwards debrief the individual or the group, perhaps in the form of asking them whether they thought it went well or whether they would change things next time.

Instructing is tiring, not just physically but more importantly because a yacht skipper has to be continually concerned about the welfare of his crew. Being confined with strangers while being considerate, fair and pleasant as well as instructing is exhausting. As you become more experienced the yachting decisions become easier as does dealing with the people. But at the point where it becomes too easy, stop or in your over-confidence, you may lose the enthusiasm and energy that make a good course.

ACCIDENTS

Every yachtsman has made errors of judgement. What matters is that you spot the error early and remain in control while you try to solve the problem. In the worst situations, a combination of circumstances may result in loss of the yacht or a crew member. The subsequent enquiry will be asking you searching questions about how you tried to retrieve the situation.

You will have to write a report of the accident which will be sent to the Marine Accident Investigation branch. Appendix 4 lists the details to be included. Hand in the report as soon as possible, and remember honesty is the best policy.

THE START YACHTING COURSE

Start Yachting is an introductory course for complete beginners to sailing. Tuition is on board a cruising yacht.

Their is no minimum age limit but centres should ensure that a lifejacket of the correct size is available, if necessary.

After gaining a Start Yachting certificate, students can progress by taking a Competent Crew course.

To complete the Competent Crew course the student will need to receive tuition afloat on a cruising yacht over a further three days and two nights, or two full weekends.

Students who hold a keelboat certificate under the National Sailing Scheme can gain a Competent Crew certificate by completing a further three days or two weekends on a cruising yacht.

Note: the sailing requirements for the keelboat courses exceed those for Start Yachting and even Competent Crew, but the student will have had less cruising experience and possibly be light on the recommended miles for entry to Day skipper.

In these cases centres may wish to advise the student that they should gain further experience on board a yacht.

Course
The Instructor/student ratio must not exceed 5:1

The course must last two days or equivalent

Instructors
The course may be delivered by the following:

a. Cruising Instructor

b. Yachtmaster Instructor

c. Yachtmaster Examiner

THE COMPETENT CREW COURSE
This course is for the newcomer to sailing or for someone who has a little dinghy sailing but no cruising experience.

Their is no minimum age limit but centres should ensure that a lifejacket of the correct size is available, if necessary.

As well as gaining instruction it is to be hoped that students will want to continue cruising after their course. The skipper's personality and skill in handling the crew will be remembered as much as his skill in handling the boat. A happy ship will gain converts to cruising who might well return for further courses.

Before the course, it is important that the skipper checks that everyone has sufficient and adequate clothing and waterproofs for the cruise. Most sailing centres hire or have oilskins available.

The instructor should remember that a small yacht is a very strange environment to the beginner and should therefore not attempt a long passage on the first day. This just results in extreme fatigue and usually seasickness. Day one should start with an initial safety briefing, but do not make this too long as the course is essentially practical and people have arrived to go sailing.

Having given the initial safety briefing and got underway, it is worth spending some time on simple manoeuvres such as coming alongside, to allow the crew to become used to moving around the boat. Soon after that, having set sail, give everybody a short turn at the helm while they settle down and enjoy the yacht under sail. Organise a reef and a headsail change at an early stage.

Ensure that all these tasks are carried out absolutely correctly. It will not only teach the crew good practice but save you having to re-instruct later on. Seamanship is often about saving yourself work. For example, coiling a warp correctly is less effort than untangling a lot of spaghetti in a cockpit locker. Putting a reef in correctly while in sheltered water is less trouble than putting it in hurriedly and having to re-adjust it later in the open sea.

Most crews will be pretty tired after a day of this sort of exercise and it is important not to continue too late. An evening moored or at anchor is a good opportunity to go through the day's events pointing out the things that were done well and those which require improvement. It is also a good time to make a start on knots.

Although this is not a navigation course, most crews are interested in chartwork and like to become involved in the navigational decisions.

During the next four days the instructor should organise interesting and varied passages, which introduce the beginner to the pleasures of yacht cruising and also cover the syllabus. Try to moor in as many different and interesting places as possible. Sailing from marina to marina is far less valuable than spending say, one night at anchor another on pile moorings and another on a swinging mooring.

Time will have to be allocated for specific teaching sessions. For example, the man overboard procedure must be demonstrated. This should be an effective and organised illustration of what you are actually going to do when somebody falls over the side. The RYA does not recommend any specific method for demonstration on this course but you are asked to consider what you would tell the coroner if he asked you why you didn't use the engine.

Another important session is on helmsmanship and sailing. This is probably best achieved by spending a couple of hours sailing around a short triangular course, giving each of the crew a chance to helm. Essentially you are employing the same method of sailing instruction as that used on basic dinghy sailing courses.

The dinghy must be launched at least once during the five days. Beginners often learn quicker if they are given the chance to try rowing on their own or with one other in a sheltered and safe place. Everyone knows what they should be doing when rowing. It is simply a matter of practice rather than a lot of instruction.

The RYA cruising scheme has credibility both nationally and internationally and high standards should be maintained at all times. This is particularly relevant in harbour and good sailing centres make a point of ensuring that their yachts always look smart and well organised when moored. It is also important that the normal courtesies are observed when mooring alongside other yachts. A great deal of damage can be done to a centre's reputation by inconsiderate behaviour in harbour.

Four night hours should be included during the week. These do not have to be continuous, they may be in two sessions. Night sailing for beginners is much more interesting if there are plenty of lights and ships to see. A port entry at night is often a high point of the trip.

Every session should end with a debrief. It is well worth rounding off a passage with a discussion of the events of the day, even though it might be late in the evening.

One of the pleasures of teaching the Competent Crew course is watching the students' apprehension change to enjoyment as the confusion of ropes and equipment turns into an organised system for sailing the yacht efficiently. A skillful instructor who runs a well balanced week will not only receive letters of thanks but also may meet the same students coming back year after year.

Standards for the award of a certificate

Most people who have been instructed well should be able to pass the Competent Crew certificate. Indeed, if they have not been able to complete the course the instructor should seriously consider whether he has taught them effectively. Students who are not awarded the certificate have usually not completed the course because:

1. In spite of the efforts of the instructor they have just not enjoyed sailing. Not everyone gets the same enjoyment out of the sport.

2. They were completely incapacitated by seasickness throughout the whole week, and therefore gained no pleasure from the cruise.

3. They were one of the very few catastrophically incapable or clumsy people who is really more of a danger than a help on board.

THE DAY SKIPPER COURSE

This is a beginner's skippering course which does for skippers what the Competent Crew does for crews. It concentrates on the two most difficult aspects of skippering a yacht for the beginner: pilotage and boat handling. The itinerary is usually rather different from the other two courses, in that passage making is much less important.

People who have never skippered a yacht, however experienced they might be as crew, should attend this course. All skippers know that there is an immense difference between being the mate and being the person in charge. The course introduces the problems and responsibilities of being in charge of a yacht and how to cope with the common difficulties.

The minimum age limit for award of a certificate is 16.

The suggested minimum pre-course experience is that which would be gained on the Competent Crew course. The assumed knowledge is defined as basic navigation and sailing ability. The navigation ability should be that required to draw an EP, have a reasonable idea of tidal heights and tidal streams, basic chartwork and seamanship. The Day Skipper shorebased course obviously gives ideal training.

Sailing ability can be defined as being able to sail a boat around a triangular course one leg of which is to windward. Gybing should not be a surprise.

In general, over estimation of ability is not too much of a problem on this course. Most Day Skippers accept that they have to start at the beginning and are very pleased to be taught the basics.

Day One. After the initial briefing (Appendix 3), it is worth starting the day with manoeuvres such as coming alongside and power handling. These can be followed by sailing exercises and deck work, reefing and changing headsails. Do not attempt long passages at this stage. The yacht should be moored up in good time for an extensive debrief. It will probably be necessary to revise the navigation part of the syllabus. Passage preparation for the next day is a useful way of covering the main points. A checklist will ensure that all the important points are covered.

You should constantly bear in mind that it is the student's first experience of skippering a yacht. To the newcomer both sailing the yacht and the navigation involved can be fairly confusing with all the different problems to consider.

Sailing instructors usually have very good anticipation so it is important that they remain patient with beginners who have to think things through slowly. It may be obvious to the instructor which sails to put up or where the channel goes next but to someone without any background knowledge these decisions can be quite taxing.

The trainee skippers never take total responsibility for the yacht, but during the week the day to day decision making can be gradually delegated to them. Each student should be given the opportunity of skippering the yacht at least once. In areas where the harbours are close together it is usually possible to give each student two passages as skipper. Attempts at say, entering harbours for the first time should be successful, so ensure that although the trainee skipper is giving instructions to the crew you have discussed with him any potential problems which might arise. The crew of the day therefore see the skipper as being in charge, but the instructor has foreseen and averted any serious problems. Much of the debriefing is done while the yacht is underway. Keep everyone informed as to what is happening and why.

As in the Competent Crew course, debrief the skipper at the end of each passage in front of the rest of the crew. This is usually done sitting around the chart in the saloon.

Pilotage

Pilotage is one of the most difficult skills for the beginner to master and can be challenging even for experienced skippers. An effective and well worked out pilotage plan is essential. Trainee skippers will need help as they will find it difficult to identify the important features to look out for and the times during the entry or departure when it is essential that the navigator is on deck. We have all seen yachts entering harbour with badly prepared navigators dashing down to the chart table and missing essential navigation marks. Once the yacht is off track it takes even more skill to identify where it is and direct it back on course.

When entering a harbour there are certain points, usually when passing navigation marks or when the course changes, when the position of the yacht is known fairly precisely. It is vital at these times that the navigator makes use of this certainty of position to identify the next mark or any other features that are necessary. If a yacht's position is known, then with a chart and a compass, any feature can be identified. If things are going too fast one of these known positions is a good place to stop. If pilotage starts to go wrong, it is usually quicker and easier to go back to a known position than, for example, to try to establish a position with a three point fix with hand bearing compass, particularly if the yacht is travelling at any speed in confined tidal waters.

Skippers who are good at pilotage often appear to be doing very little, because they have pre-planned each move and are always one jump ahead. Skippers who are poor at pilotage are usually in a panic because they are always one step behind. Weak pilotage is a common reason for failing the Yachtmaster examination so sailing instructors should make a point of teaching this part of the syllabus particularly carefully. There is a tendency to forget what a familiar harbour looks like through the eyes of someone who has never been there.

Boat handling

Do not aim so much for success first time and every time but rather an understanding of the principles concerned. An essential element is tidal awareness. Manoeuvres should be practised in various conditions of wind and tide. Boat handling practice is very hard work for the crew so little and often is probably of more use than protracted sessions. Concentrate on control of boat speed and being on the correct point of sail.

If the man overboard is taught under sail a method should be used which involves a tack rather than a gybe. If the engine is used the quick stop method is recommended. (See Appendix 2). A sailing instructor should be able to give a convincing demonstration of either of these methods in virtually any conditions.

Meteorology

Keep the meteorology practical. Use the shipping forecast and observations of the sky to make practical decisions. It is usually unnecessary to record the weather forecast for North Utsire when making short passages in the Solent. Sailing instructors are usually very good at using forecasts for passage planning and this part of the course is one of the most valuable for the student.

Rules of the road

Day Skippers should know the IRPCS well enough to be able to identify and avoid collision situations.

Most passages are in areas where ships have right of way because they are constrained by their draughts. Providing they are clear as to how to take avoiding action the precise identification of the type of ship is not essential. An exception to this is the tug towing which often demands different avoiding action.

The basic sailing rules must be known.

In most areas this part of the syllabus can be taught as the course progresses.

Maintenance

Many of the problems which disable yachts are due to lack of routine maintenance. Students should be made aware of the need for observation, checking, cleaning and replacement of the yacht's equipment. The engine requires particular attention. It is not necessary or even desirable to set students in front of the engine with a tool kit, it is more important to demonstrate engine checks and simple maintenance.

Wind awareness

A number of students on Day Skipper courses have poor wind awareness. Sailing instructors should insist on good sail trim at all times and remind the crew that a course alteration will involve an alteration to the sails.

Standards

Day Skipper certificates are awarded to students who have learnt the general principles of skippering a yacht and will go on to become Coastal Skipper standard.

They can undertake short passages by day in familiar waters having listened to the forecasts and worked out the tidal streams. They have basic tidal awareness when boat handling and can attempt basic power and sailing manoeuvres. If they have to attempt a mooring, man overboard or coming alongside several times it is through lack of practice rather than through lack of understanding.

Day Skippers have sufficient knowledge to avoid trouble and know their limitations. Good yacht skippers (and instructors) can identify their own weaknesses.

PASS OR FAIL?

Student A

No previous courses. Has sailed as crew with friends on a one week channel cruise. Rather over confident and passed the evening class Day Skipper shorebased course with flying colours. On the first day found sailing to windward difficult and became disorientated on tacking. Chartwork good but tended to navigate chart table and not observe, especially during pilotage. Improved on this during the week. Tended to pick up man overboard on broad reach. Power handling better but a bit fast. Confused by use of springs on lee berth.

Decision

All sections signed except 9, 12 and 13. Recommended to attend dinghy or keelboat courses to improve sailing skills. His biggest problem is over confidence.

Student B

Owns a dinghy. Has not attended shorebased course but has read some navigation. Competent Crew last year. Good natural sailor. Rather hesitant and very cautious under power. Theory weak but improved through course. Navigation a bit hit and miss but understood basics after intensive tuition.

Decision

Pass after much intensive tuition on navigation. Natural sailors tend to pick up the rest of the course quickly and can think on their feet.

Students C and D

Husband and Wife team. Own 26ft bilge keel. Some local sailing. Both attended shorebased course and passed easily.

Student C

Husband. Always takes command. Tends to shout when in difficulties. Very conscientious but rather defensive when errors made. Good practical navigator. Cautious sailor (drops sails early). Tends to overtrim sails but has reasonable idea of wind direction.

Student D

Wife. Keen and quick to learn. Very receptive to instruction. Found skippering difficult while husband on deck. (Instructor had to ensure his instructions not repeated as orders by husband). Worked out problems as they arose. Good navigator. Sailing weak at first but improving rapidly. Pilotage a bit hesitant (took a very long time with frequent stops). Much more confident by end of week.

Decision

C. Pass with careful debrief. The instructor is not assessing personality but can demonstrate how to get the best from a crew, and how a yacht is controlled with minimum fuss and shouting.

Technically he was safe and completed all the sections of the course adequately.

D. Very marginal pass. A pass would give great confidence and improve her enjoyment of yachting enormously. A fail would be demoralising and might put her off for good. A difficult decision but the speed of improvement should continue and she knows her limitations.

Families often want to sail together but actually learn faster apart.

THE COASTAL SKIPPER COURSE

This course, like the Day Skipper is primarily a training week but with more assessment of ability and potential.

The minium age limit for issue of a certificate is 17.

It is not a course for the beginner, hence the suggested requirement of two days as skipper. One or possibly both of these days might have been gained on a previous course, but the experience requirement of 15 days has been introduced to discourage trainee skippers whose entire experience has been during RYA courses. The inside cover of G15 warns against attempting a course which is too advanced. It is easier to direct someone to the correct course at the outset than persuade them halfway through that they are below standard.

Most yachtsmen are aspiring Yachtmasters so we are inevitably going to find a few who attend a Coastal Skipper course before they are ready. The answer is to give them an honest, positive, individual debrief after a day or two to let them know how they stand in terms of the scheme. If this is handled with tact there is no reason why the week should not be successful and constructive. The spirit of the scheme is to instruct everyone to his or her best ability. Certificates are secondary to this. Sailing is, after all, a recreation and the reason for attending courses is to become more proficient, to worry less and therefore to gain more enjoyment.

The itinerary should be chosen carefully to include longer passages but also to give sufficient time for boat handling and pilotage.

Skippers at this level should be able to plan a passage and make most decisions without frequent help. The instructor can and should give every encouragement and assistance if asked for advice but should also allow the skipper of the day to take responsibility for implementing his plan. The skill of running this course is deciding to what extent it is constructive to allow mistakes to be made. For example, in some circumstances running aground can be a very useful and instructive exercise. All skippers will ground sooner or later, doing so under instruction is a good way to learn. Failing to notice that a yacht is being swept downtide of its destination also teaches an important lesson but could waste several hours which could be more usefully employed.

Boat handling in a confined space involves the greatest level of anticipation. The good instructor talks his student out of problems and only rarely takes the helm away. Again the problem is 'to what extent is this mistake useful?'

The Coastal Skipper course covers all the practical and theoretical knowledge for the Coastal Skipper and Yachtmaster examinations. There is a lot of instruction to cover and, with longer passages, the days are extended and tiring. Sailing centres should be aware of the dangers of expecting instructors to run this course week after week without a break.

Passage planning and passage making

At least one passage should involve a watch system and if possible the yacht should be taken sufficiently far offshore to involve drawing real EP's on the chart. Of course the actual decisions are dependent on the strength of the crew and the weather conditions.

In the event of heavy weather the instructor has an ideal opportunity to demonstrate the techniques of strong wind sailing. Inexperienced skippers gain a great deal from being shown that a well organised, sound yacht in sheltered water can continue cruising.

Each student should be asked to skipper a passage which includes pilotage in or out of harbour, and one of the port entries should be at night.

Boat handling

Coastal Skippers should be able to continue cruising under sail in the event of engine failure. This means sailing in fairly confined spaces, and picking up moorings. The man overboard should be picked up under sail as well as under power.

Before we consider the RYA Cruising scheme an unqualified success we should remember that mechanical failure is the most common cause of lifeboat rescues to auxiliary sailing yachts. The RNLI would be saved a lot of trouble if all yacht skippers were proficient sailors.

Under power, the course should include as many different berthing situations as possible preferably including a fore and aft or pile mooring. Tidal awareness is essential.

With all boat handling the important skill is positioning the yacht correctly so that the pontoon, mooring or man overboard is approached with the yacht in the right orientation to wind and/or tide. Identifying the starting position is often the hardest part to teach. It is easy to speed up or slow down a yacht on a close reach as it approaches a mooring buoy. It is much more difficult to position the yacht so that when it is pointed at the buoy it is close reaching. When picking up wind with tide moorings or a man overboard it is essential that the mainsail can flap. This should be tested as the yacht approaches by releasing the mainsheet. If the main draws even when the sheet is fully out then the line of approach should be altered by steering further downwind. By using this method to check the point of sail during manoeuvres, even very inexperienced sailors can reduce speed close to a man or buoy in the water.

In strong winds more skill is required to judge the leeway made as the yacht slows down. The starting position is further upwind. The same applies to wind with tide moorings in a strong tidal stream. Here it is a case of keeping the mooring on a transit as the yacht glides towards it, still close reaching but pointing uptide.

The man overboard recovery technique is, of course, unaffected by tidal stream.

Wind against tide moorings require less skill. The speed is easier to control as the yacht sails under jib or bare poles from an upwind position. It is simply a matter of deciding to drop the mainsail and choosing a suitable clear space upwind of the mooring to do so. Where there is doubt in wind across tide situations it is usually safer to drop the main. One way of checking the approach is to sail past the mooring in the direction the yacht will lie when secured. As you close the buoy, release the main. If it flaps keep it up, if not lower it.

Remember it is the principles which are important. There will not be time to make everyone a first class boat handler. The best you can do is ensure that your students acquire sufficient knowledge and understanding to become Yachtmasters with practice.

Efficient sailing

Many cruising Yachtsmen are vague about the correct setting for sail controls such as the mainsheet traveller, jib fairleads, kicking strap and adjustable backstay. Sailing Instructors should always endeavour to set up the yacht efficiently, using tell tales when necessary.

Pilotage

Pilotage is most difficult at night when the yacht has to be kept in a channel with few marks surrounded by a large expanse of water. It is easiest by day in a deep channel clearly marked either by the land or navigation buoys.

Picking out and identifying lights by night may be easy for the experienced instructor but can be very taxing for the beginner. Make sure they are given time and not pressurised. If they are disorientated, stop and establish the position of the yacht, identification then simply involves a chart and hand bearing compass.

Most instructors endeavour to enter new ports each year both to add extra personal interest and to remind themselves of the skills required to enter a strange harbour.

Meteorology

Coastal Skippers should be able to interpret all the available forecasts to make practical decisions on offshore passages. Because the passages are longer than those at Day Skipper level, more information and interpretation is required.

IRPCS

A knowledge to the level of the Coastal Skipper shorebased course is required.

End of the course

During the last day it is worth giving the students a further chance to try manoeuvres or parts of the syllabus that they were unhappy about on their passages.

PASS OR FAIL

At the end of the course the instructor does not have to decide whether or not a student is up to the required standard for the award of a Coastal Skipper certificate. He has to decide whether or not the student has sufficient understanding of the problems associated with taking a yacht to sea to improve his own ability so that, after further experience, he will be competent to skipper a yacht safely.

A course completion certificate must not be awarded to any student who shows reluctance to accept full responsibility for the yacht and her crew when he is acting as skipper. A certificate must not be awarded to any student who suffers from seasickness which makes it impossible for him to skipper a yacht effectively. Neither must a certificate be awarded to anyone whose basic knowledge or skill in seamanship, boat handling or navigation would make him a positive danger as a skipper.

Student E

Very keen to gain Yachtmaster has attended Competent Crew and Day Skipper practical courses and all shorebased including Ocean. Anxious to learn, not a natural sailor but can think out manoeuvres. Gets there eventually but has to work out wind direction at times. Theory excellent but tends to navigate the chart table instead of the boat. This improved throughout the course. Made a lot of progress throughout the five days. Knows her limitations.

Decision

Marginal pass with honest debrief about sailing ability. Would probably fail Coastal Skipper practical exam until more sailing experience gained, and needs to be told this. Her positive attitude to her mistakes was encouraging.

Student F

Has sailed as mate with sail training organisation and in various smaller yachts as crew. Coastal Skipper shorebased course. Excellent as crew very willing and cheerful. Boat handling under power and sail occasionally lacks tidal awareness particularly in tight corners. Has difficulty judging boat speed when approaching man overboard and moorings. Quite a good sailor once underway. Organises the yacht well.

Decision

All sections signed except 5, 6 and 8. Encouraged to gain more skippering experience. This candidate could be awarded the Day Skipper certificate providing the appropriate sections are covered.

PRACTICAL AND THEORY COURSES FOR PEOPLE WITH DISABILITIES

All RYA training courses are open to people with disabilities.

There are teaching and enablement issues that sometimes have to be addressed, but all these perceived hurdles disappear when common sense, good practice and seamanship are employed. There is no better source of information about prospective students than students themselves. The key to good practice is, without doubt, good communication.

Classroom work is usually only affected by sensory disability, e.g. visual impairment or deafness. Such problems are normally anticipated by the student who will provide additional people to interpret or assist. Please ensure that any physical restrictions the building would impose on wheelchair users are known to you and explained prior to a course.

Practical courses provide an initial challenge for the instructor. People with visual impairment benefit from the use of an audio compass which, given notice, RYA Sailability can provide. Deaf students need good light to lip read (a torch will suffice at night) and a dry marker pen and a sheet of white plastic is a practical asset.

Students with mobility problems are often unable to move about the boat. This is not a barrier to the successful completion of the course. All students must be able to demonstrate their ability to complete the whole syllabus, but this can be achieved by proxy. A candidate who cannot perform a task directly must be able to satisfactorily direct a third party to achieve that task on their behalf. It is worth bearing in mind that this method of achieving a task requires more skill than the operation itself as the candidate has to possess good communication and teaching skills as well as knowing how to undertake the manoeuvre. The instructor will soon find many new uses for the bosun's chair, mainsheet tackle and single point moorings!

The 'special endorsements' line of a certificate should be treated with care. Do not list any disability unless it affects the holder's aptitude directly in the handling of a vessel. The prosthesis that gives the user complete function is of no consequence. However a visually impaired person may well have the endorsement 'Requires visual assistance when at sea'.

RYA Sailability is always on hand to answer any questions or give advice. Their telephone number is 0238 060 4247.

SHOREBASED SCHEME

RECOGNITION OF SHOREBASED TRAINING CENTRES

The majority of shorebased teaching centress are adult education colleges or institutes.

Shorebased courses are also organised by yacht clubs, privately owned sailing centres and correspondence colleges.

It is the RYA's policy to recognise any college or institute of a Local Education Authority and any RYA affiliated club to conduct shorebased courses, provided that satisfactory evidence can be shown as to the suitability of the course instructor(s). It is the responsibility of the local authority Principal to satisfy himself as to the proposed instructor's ability to teach.

Centres wishing to apply for recognition should contact the RYA for an application form. The form asks for details of the sailing and teaching experience of the proposed tutors.

In the case of privately-owned centres, the RYA must be satisfied that the accommodation available for teaching is suitable and that the instructor has the appropriate sailing and teaching qualifications.

It is not normally the policy of the RYA to limit the number of recognised centres in any area but recognition may be refused on the grounds that there are already sufficient centres to meet the need for courses in an area and the recognition of a further centres would be likely to reduce class numbers to an uneconomic level.

Correspondence schools

Schools that wish to offer shorebased courses for the award of RYA certificates of satisfactory completion must hold recognition as Correspondence Schools from the RYA. Centres applying to the RYA will incur extra costs for checking the suitability of training material.

Course materials

Each student must be issued with the current RYA students' shorebased pack, which includes the assessment papers, charts, electronic chart plotter and a course notebook. Access to the current Practice Navigation Tables published by the RYA is also a requirement.

Electronic chart plotter

The minimum requirement for student contact time with the electronic chart plotter is:

• Day Skipper 2 hours   • Coastal Skipper/Yachtmaster 3 hours

This contact time can be at home or in the classroom. If in the classroom - a maximum of 3 students to a computer at any time.

Instructors can obtain an instructors' pack, details of which are included on the Account Holders price list available to recognised centres.

In order to avoid delays, teaching materials may be ordered by a recognised centre or instructor on a sale or return basis before the course starts. To qualify for credit, the papers must be returned to the RYA in their original sealed pack within 30 days of receipt.

Marking

The assessment papers are marked by the instructor using standard answers and chart overlays provided by the RYA. Student numbers and pass/fail rates are monitored regularly by the RYA; instructors are expected to maintain records of students' progress each year.

Communications

Two addresses are held on the RYA database for recognised shorebased centres. One is the address of the centre where the courses are held. The other is the correspondence address to which newsletters and information are sent. The two addresses can be the same. This information is updated yearly unless any advice of address change is received in the interim.

Advertising

Only recognised training centres may use the name of the RYA in advertising.

If a centre is involved in other boating activities which are not recognised by the RYA, care should be taken that advertising does not imply that these other activities are in any way sanctioned by the RYA .

QUALIFICATION OF SHOREBASED INSTRUCTORS

Navigation courses

Shorebased instructors must be experienced yachtsmen who hold a shorebased Instructor or Yachtmaster Instructor or Examiner qualification. In addition, those wishing to run the Yachtmaster Ocean Shorebased should also hold the Ocean Certificate of Competence.

Each winter, one day conferences are held at various locations throughout the UK to inform instructors of new developments and to exchange information about the scheme.

SRC, Radar and Diesel Engine Maintenance courses

Before teaching these, instructors must have attended a training course. Please contact the RYA for details.

CONDUCT OF SHOREBASED COURSES

RYA shorebased courses shall be run only by establishments recognised by the RYA.

RYA recognition depends on:

1. There being a suitably qualified instructor.
2. A suitably equipped teaching room which will allow all the students to do chartwork simultaneously and has computer and audio visual facilities.

The Principal of the centre is responsible for ensuring that adequate standards of tuition are maintained.

Each course should involve a minimum of forty hours teaching and allow sufficient time for assessment papers. twenty four two-hour evening sessions is usual for night centres. A five day intensive course is possible for Day Skipper. For Coastal Skipper a minimum of seven days is usually required.

TEACHING THE SHOREBASED COURSES

The purpose of the shorebased scheme is to provide an opportunity for would be skippers and crews to learn about subjects such as navigation and meteorology, the principles of which are best taught in a classroom. The shorebased instructor should constantly bear in mind that the courses are part of an overall scheme involving practical tuition, consolidation by experience and examinations. Where a shorebased centre does not have direct contact with the practical scheme there is sometimes a tendency to regard shorebased certificates as the end product of a yachtsman's education. The full value of the shorebased scheme is only realised by applying the skills and knowledge learnt in a classroom to practical situations on board a yacht.

There is no compulsory certification for the skippers of small pleasure craft in this country. The RYA hopes that through its national training schemes yachtsmen will be motivated to achieve high standards by joining a voluntary system. The shorebased courses are constantly updated with information from the coastguard, rescue services, sailing centres and private yachtsmen. The syllabus is revised every five years, and a new set of assessment exercises is written each year.

Students on RYA theory courses are men and women of every age from every type of background and range from the highly academic to those with no formal education since leaving centre. The instructor must organise effective, pleasant and successful tuition for everyone in the class. Ensuring that each lesson is worthwhile and interesting involves careful planning. Unplanned lessons tend to turn into long and boring lectures. Good lecturers ensure that each session involves a number of varied activities to maintain the interest of the students.

GETTING THE STUDENTS ON THE RIGHT COURSE

The most common problem here is students enrolling on the Coastal Skipper/Yachtmaster course when they have little or no previous navigational experience. It is important that the advertising for the shorebased centre makes it quite clear that the Coastal Skipper course is not for beginners, and this should be reinforced on the enrolment evening. The inside cover of the log book which summarises the courses is intended to clarify the experience required. Suitable wording for an advertisement is given below.

Day Skipper Sail/Motor Cruising.

This is an elementary course in basic seamanship, navigation and meteorology, suitable for beginners and people with little experience in yachts.

Coastal Skipper/Yachtmaster Offshore Sail/Motor Cruising.

A more advanced course in navigation and meteorology, suitable for students who have already completed the elementary course, or who have a background of cruising or offshore racing experience. The course is definitely not suitable for beginners.

Yachtmaster Ocean Sail/Motor Cruising.

A course in astro-navigation and world-wide meteorology. A knowledge of terrestrial navigation and basic meteorology up to the standard of the Coastal Skipper/Yachtmaster Offshore shorebased course is assumed.

Time spent being honest with potential students and ensuring that they are on the right course will save a lot of difficulties and unhappiness later on. Exercise 1 of the Coastal Skipper/Yachtmaster assessment papers is intended as a guideline to the standard required at the beginning of the course.

PLANNING THE OVERALL COURSE

The instructor should make out an overall plan of the entire course. The syllabus in the log book gives the minimum time allocation for each topic which will assist in the course plan. An example of a week by week plan is given below. It is of course important that each student has completed all the exercises and assessments satisfactorily. This means that they must all be marked, though with the short exercises this is often best done in the classroom. The RYA exercises are not intended to be the only questions that the students should attempt during the course, instructors should provide their own problems based on the syllabus to ensure that every student really understands each topic. Preparing these exercises is time consuming and hard work but they can, of course, be used in subsequent years.

COASTAL SKIPPER/YACHTMASTER OFFSHORE EVENING CLASS – A TYPICAL PROGRAMME

All Classes 1900 - 2100

Week	Topics/Examples	Exercise
1.	Introduction. Information. Basic chartwork. Symbols.	Ex A
2.	Basic chartwork. Dead reckoning & estimated position.	Ex 1
3.	DR and EP continued. Magnetic compass.	Ex B
4.	Chartwork exercises. Deck log.	Ex 3
5.	Position fixing, sources of position lines.	Ex 3
6.	Tides (rise and fall). Echo sounders.	Ex 2
7.	Tides (Solent and Channel).	Ex 2
8.	Tidal streams.	Ex C
9.	Chartwork exercises.	Ex 3 & 4
10.	Shaping courses.	Ex 4
11.	Pilotage lights and clearing bearings.	Ex 5 Ex D
12.	Passage planning. Strategy.	Ex 6
13.	Passage planning exercises	Ex 6
14.	Electronic Navigation	Ex 5
15.	Safety at sea. Stability. Customs.	Ex H
16.	VHF radio. Chartwork. Meteorology.	
17.	Anchoring. Meteorology.	Ex F
18.	Meteorology. Fog Navigation.	Ex F
19.	Chartwork. Meteorology.	
20.	Revision VHF tests.	
21.	Revision.	
22.	General chartwork - Collision regulations revise.	Ex 7,E & G
23.	Meteorology.	assessment paper 8
24.	Exercise 9 Collision regulations.	assessment paper 9
25.	Exercise 10 Chartwork.	assessment paper 10
26.	Discussion. Results. Film.	

In addition, homework will be set as required throughout the course and students will be expected to learn the International Regulations for the Prevention of Collisions at Sea during home study.

Regular circulars from the RYA keep instructors up to date on new developments in yachting and the emphasis of the questions reflects this. Instructors should be constantly updating their material to ensure that they are not teaching outmoded topics or subjects which are not included in the syllabus.

LESSON PLANS

Using the overall course plan a detailed lesson plan can be constructed. Although the broad detail of this can be done well in advance, it is worth leaving some flexibility to allow for topics or problems which have arisen from previous sessions. For each lesson the instructor should be absolutely clear in his own mind what he wants to achieve and the points that he wants to get across. Most evening class sessions are two hours which gives an opportunity for a variety of activities, for example, a short test on collision regulations, formal lecturing including visual aids, group work on passage planning and chart work. Chart work exercises give the instructor a good opportunity to talk to individual students and identify problems.

A typical plan is shown below.

TYPICAL LESSON PLAN

Time	Activity	Notes	Vis. Aids
1900	Coll Regs test		Magnetic discs or whiteboard
1910	Return EP Questions Ex 3	Still some tidal stream problems	Ex 3 Answers Acetate
1930	Lecture on Course to Steer Note taking	Intro: why shape course. Navigating in future (EP in past) Story of skipper confusing Fl5 St Cats with Fl10 Anvil Pt because no course x-channel shaping. Required even with GPS. Lecture: Drawing the Δ. Need to know:	
		1 Position 2 Boat Speed (estimate) may change 3 Time (don't plot too early) 4 Tidal Streams 5 Variation 6 Deviation 7 Leeway (EP leeway before you pick up pencil Course to steer leeway after pencil down)	Pre-prepared acetate/Powerpoint
		Draw Δ (may have to go over tidal streams) (remember arrows) 1 pint beer penalty for anyone joining end of tide vector to destination	Blank Acetate Breton Plotter Dividers Pens
		Draw Δ on chart acetate to show actual situation where course required Passages using two tides	Copy acetate of section of chart

2000	Questions	Conclusion: Why course to steer What info required Draw Δ again Common faults	Pre-prepared Acetate/Powerpoint
2010	Break	Talk to John, Phil & Jenny re homework - are they struggling?	
2020	Start RYA Ex4	Help individuals as necessary	
2055	Set Homework	Complete Exercise 4 Read Nav. Instruments before next session Reminder of visit to Coastguard	

Learning

Certain parts of the RYA shorebased courses require straight learning of facts. As people get older this often becomes more difficult, but with good instruction it can be fairly painless. The instructor should first identify those parts of the syllabus which require significant amounts of learning rather than learning and understanding; for example the collision regulations, buoyage, parts of the boat etc. Little, often and early is a good way to approach these topics. Short tests lasting say 10 minutes at the beginning of each session motivate the students and ensure that they retain the facts. It is worth getting students to write down the answers rather than have one student (usually the same one every time) calling out the answer. The instructor will also get an idea as to which students have grasped the subject. Visual aids are very helpful when learning a new subject, and the RYA provides OHP acetates and other materials which can be used both for teaching and for testing. The students can be encouraged to make their own visual aids such as flipcards. Making your own cards is a much more effective way of learning than memorising facts from manufactured material.

While subjects like the IRPCS are vital to the yachtsman, it is important not to use up too much teaching time on these pure learning subjects at the expense of the topics which students find hard to understand. It is therefore worth asking the students to learn the regulations at home and give them short tests rather than spending time in class going through each rule in detail.

Understanding

The hard part of teaching the courses, and the most interesting, is those which require understanding. The main topics which require particular attention in this respect are:

tidal heights	passage planning
tidal streams	meteorology
EPs	pilotage
course to steer	

It is virtually impossible to teach these subjects effectively purely by lecturing. The students must be involved in activities such as chartwork or listening to forecasts etc. so that they can understand by actually doing.

Chartwork

A subject such as chartwork involves careful development of a theme. Don't assume that the students have good mathematical knowledge or will find simple chartwork easy. Most students associate the course with chartwork and are disappointed if the chart is not used from an early stage of the course. Chartwork requires constant practice and so the instructor must be equipped with plenty of examples in addition to the RYA questions to reinforce the concepts. Chartwork answers these questions:

1. Where am I? or
2. Where do I go from here? or
3. Have I an adequate margin of safety from navigational hazards?

Pilotage is essentially answering these questions but closer to the land.

Tides

Calculating tidal heights is probably the most difficult part of the syllabus to teach and to learn. By an unfortunate coincidence this part of the course often occurs just at the end of the first term and can discourage students from returning in January. It is vital that the instructor really understands how to work out the tidal heights for primary and secondary ports and understands when this information is needed. Tidal height problems answer one of two questions:

either 1. When?

or 2. How high?

In all problems you are either given the height and asked the time or given the time and asked the height.

Accuracy

In shorebased courses a high level of accuracy is always required. On the practical course the instructor will explain those occasions when great accuracy is needed, such as waiting to cross a marina sill, and when an approximation is adequate. The role of the shorebased instructor is to arm the yachtsman with sufficient knowledge to cope with any navigational problems that he might meet at sea, and this may involve working to a great accuracy.

The same principle applies to chartwork. In many situations along the coast it is unnecessary to draw accurate triangles, or indeed draw triangles at all. However should the visibility drop then the ability to navigate quickly and accurately is essential. The significance of this is brought home very strongly on practical courses.

Tidal streams

Tidal streams are difficult because they are constantly changing and the data often has to be interpolated. Practically, most yachtsmen take the data for springs or neaps or halfway between the two. Initially it might be worth teaching tidal streams like this to emphasise the importance of the actual chartwork rather than getting too involved in the mathematics. Later the computation of rates table can be used to give more accurate results for those occasions when you really do need accurate chartwork.

Meteorology

Teaching meteorology is difficult because most courses happen at night and many people with indoor jobs do not really observe the weather . Weather is much more understandable if looked at over a period of a few days. Probably the most understandable weather feature is the cold front. A description of the conditions before and after a cold front should be recognisable to everybody, and cold fronts will cross the country at regular intervals throughout the winter. The people who can relate this subject most clearly to yachting are not meteorologists but full-time practical instructors. For tutors who are having problems with this part of the syllabus it might be worth inviting a practical instructor to explain how he makes his five day passage planning decisions based on the weather forecasts at the beginning of the course.

Make meteorology as practical as possible. If an interesting weather feature is crossing your area, take a few minutes at the beginning or end of the class to explain what is happening. Weather faxes and newspaper synoptic charts make excellent and relevant visual aids.

A Yachtmaster has sufficient understanding of the available information to decide whether to undertake an offshore passage and can predict the likely problems over the next few days.

A Day Skipper can decide whether to undertake a day sail in familiar waters.

Avoid becoming too technical, the word yacht should be mentioned regularly.

Electronic navigation and use of the chart plotter software

This needs to be integrated throughout the chartwork and passage planning elements of the course, rather than being taught as a separate subject. Remember that when your students finish the course and go sailing, they are likely to use GPS or a chart plotter as their primary navigation tool. It is important, therefore, that they fully understand the limitations of the equipment, and are also equipped with modern methods and techniques that allow them to get the best out of their electronics. There is no requirement for all students to have simultaneous access to a computer for this element of the course, many will have access at home or in the office. You must ensure that those who don't however, do have access to a computer in the classroom.

Passage planning

Passage planning is usually a matter of deciding priorities. The RYA shorebased course notebook gives a useful checklist in order of priority. This part of the syllabus generally requires a background of sailing experience on the part of the tutor. Passage planning exercises are often more usefully tackled as a group exercise.

Pilotage

Pilotage is another subject which can be difficult to teach in the classroom. It is hard to write meaningful questions on pilotage for the shorebased course. The best that the shorebased instructor can do is to outline the general principles so that the practical instructor can put these into practice afloat. Pilotage should not be under-emphasised, it is one of the most challenging skills for yacht skippers and lack of ability in this area is a common reason for candidates failing the Yachtmaster Offshore examination. The closer a yacht is to the shore or to the bottom the harder it gets.

Stability

The teaching of stability should not be an exercise in advanced mathematics. Keep it simple, with the emphasis being on the general principles which make one boat more stable than another. A basic understanding of the angle of vanishing stability and EU Recreational Craft Directive Design Categories is also necessary to help students make the right choice when buying or chartering a boat.

Keeping the students informed

Each student must have a good idea of how they are progressing through the course and whether they are achieving a satisfactory standard. If they are finding part or all of the course difficult the instructor must identify the problem and be honest when telling the student. Every year a number of disgruntled students contact the RYA at the end of the course because they failed and did not know the reason. The problem is almost always a lack of communication between the instructor and the student. It is very unfair on the students and shows poor teaching technique if the final result is a total surprise.

If a student fails a final assessment paper then he or she may retake the test using a paper of a similar standard. This can either be a past paper or the instructor may wish to re-examine a certain point using his own questions. Students may only be re-tested if the previous course work is satisfactory. In other words, the instructor should have a fairly good idea before the final assessment papers as to whether a student has grasped the subject. If the instructor is happy with the progress so far but the student makes a number of careless errors through nerves or poor examination technique a re-sit should be offered. However, if progress has been poor throughout the course the student should be aware of this and no re-sit should be allowed. Students who find navigation difficult should not be made to feel that they are useless as sailors or that they should not go to sea. Everybody should gain some benefit from the course and everybody's knowledge of sailing should improve. All students should go away at the end of the course feeling that it was time well spent and they are better sailors as a result.

Using the RYA assessment papers

The shorebased assessment papers provide a useful monitor for the tutor and students:

1. They act as a checklist on teaching points for the instructor.

2. They enable students to assess their own progress. If students cannot do the homework they should be asking questions which will inform the instructor of their weaknesses or any lack of clarity in the tuition.

3. The final papers act as a deadline, by which time the students should know all the necessary information. The results of the final assessment papers should not be a surprise to the instructor, they should confirm what he already knows about the student. (They should not be a total surprise to the student either, as he should have been kept aware of his progress throughout the course.)

Standards for the award of the certificates

At the end of the course the instructor must decide whether the student has understood the concepts taught and has sufficient knowledge to start converting the theory into practice. By failing a candidate the instructor is saying that he or she would benefit from retaking the course.

The only assessment which has an allocated pass mark is: IRPCS   80%

End of course

By the end of the course most class members have developed friendships and the final session is often more of a social evening. Emphasis should be placed on the fact that the shorebased scheme is only a stepping stone towards becoming a proficient yachtsman. The reason that most shorebased courses occur in winter is that the knowledge gained in the classroom can be consolidated at sea in the summer. Each shorebased centre is circulated with a list of practical teaching centress which provide RYA courses under qualified supervision.

CLASSROOM TEACHING TECHNIQUES

The lecture is not always the most effective way of teaching a practical subject like sailing. However it is important that some subjects such as navigation and meteorology are taught in a classroom where there is time to ask questions and sort out problems before going to sea.

The mere statement of a fact is no guarantee that listeners have received that fact as you understand it, or will necessarily remember it for any length of time. It is important to vary your teaching technique both to maintain interest and to ensure that the points you wish to get across are actually learnt.

When classroom teaching you should bear in mind the following:

Before the course on the first session. Meet the students as they arrive, welcome them to the course. An informal start with coffee often helps you to find out who they are and their experience. If you are teaching your first course it is less daunting if you have met everyone before standing in front of them.

Learning the students' names. The instructor has a duty to learn the students' names as soon as possible. One of the easiest ways of doing this is to draw out a plan of the classroom with desks and mark where everybody sits. During the first few sessions make sure that you look at this chart and actually call people by their names when asking them questions. This makes you associate the name with the face. It is very demoralising for a student to feel that he or she is just a face without an identity to the instructor.

Find out their experience. Are they sailors or motor boaters? Are there any experts on say meteorology or fire fighting? This will help you pitch the course at the right level and might give you a useful reference later in the course.

Consider the room layout. Anything you say or do will be pointless unless your students can see and hear you. Remember that you are in charge; move furniture if necessary. Encourage students to fill lecture rooms from the front. Make sure your room is comfortable and well ventilated.

Keep lectures short. Thirty minutes is about the right length of time to maintain students' attention without testing or a break. Don't overrun.

Outline your aims at the beginning of a lecture and summarise the essential points to remember at the close. A handout stating the important facts is useful, but should not be given out until the end of the lecture. Handouts distributed at the beginning will only be read by students when they should be listening to you.

Give your lecture a structure: Introduction, Development, Summary, Test.

Link salient points to dramatic examples. It is essential that the course is taught by a tutor with small boat experience who can draw on practical examples to illustrate the syllabus. Anecdotes of the 'I won't do that again' type usually go down better than 'There I was' tales of derring- do. The class will quickly sense they are being taught by a knowledgeable and credible yachtsman without you having to remind them regularly.

Technical Language. Some of the class will understand all the technical language. Before you answer their questions on say, GPS ensure that the rest of the class know what you are talking about.

Choose your position. Where and how you stand will have an effect on your lecture. Standing behind a desk or lectern may appear more formal but puts a barrier between you and your audience. Sitting on a table at the front of the class may be too relaxed for some talks. Observe polished speakers and assess their use of body language. Don't hide behind your visual aids (see below).

Involve your audience. Speak to your audience – all of them. Don't talk to the ceiling, the floor or the wall at the back of the classroom. Try to make eye contact with every member of the audience at some stage. As alternatives to a monologue, use question and answer techniques, discussions etc. Learn and use students' names.

Avoid irritating mannerisms when teaching. Some common ones are saying OK at the end of each few sentences, playing with the chalk or blackboard pointer, pacing about unnecessarily. Detecting your mannerisms is difficult but you should be aware that they may be distracting the class.

Avoid distractions. Try to avoid distractions such as the aerobics class taking away the attention of your students from your lecture on secondary tidal heights. Prepare the room so that equipment or visual aids from previous classes do not detract from your subject matter.

Practice writing on blackboards. Prepared OHP acetates or powerpoint are preferable to copious boardwriting with your back to the students. Never talk to your blackboard, always to your students. If you are not using or have finished with a blackboard, rub it clean to avoid distraction.

Don't bluff. If you don't know the answer to a question - say so. Your students would far rather have an honest "I don't know, but I'll find out," than a bluffed answer. Having said that, you should always ensure that you have a wider knowledge of your subject than the basic facts contained in your lecture.

Don't be afraid to test. Ten questions which are immediately marked by the students themselves, will help to reinforce your teaching.

Avoid sarcasm, humiliation or rudeness. Try not to let any of your prejudices alienate members of the class. In particular avoid patronising students of a very different age group from your own and avoid sexism.

Don't try to be funny unless you are naturally witty.

Remember that some subjects may not require a lecture at all.
For example rope work is probably best done by tying the knots while the instructor goes around the class helping.

Finally, remember that your lecture will have succeeded only if all your students leave it having learnt all the important facts which you intended to communicate and are eager to learn more.

Questions

The concept of using questions in your teaching has been outlined above. Questions to the class can be used to fulfil three main purposes – to Teach, Test or Trigger more learning.

Teaching by question and answer is a technique which relies on the instructor being able to pose the right questions in order to elicit the required response. Well used, it will enable students to maintain their attention span for far longer than in a formal lecture, because they are involved.

Questioning to test is most effective if you follow the pattern of Pose – Pause – Pounce. Pose the question to the group then pause to allow the students time to think of the answer. During this time your gaze will rove around the group until you pounce on someone for the answer.

If you identify one of the group before asking the question, the others will lose attention, knowing that they are not going to be asked.

If a student doesn't know the answer, don't chastise him for it but move on to someone who does. If none of the group know the answer to something which has been covered, you clearly did not explain it properly – thus questions serve to confirm whether your teaching has been effective.

Questions can also be used to trigger more thought, possibly linking what has been covered to a future session to ensure more interest, or encouraging students to learn more outside the framework of your teaching.

Questions themselves fall into two categories - closed (or direct) which require a simple answer and open (or indirect) which lead on to more thought. In general terms, closed questions are used for simple testing, whilst open questions are more effective for teaching and triggering further thought.

Similarly, questions from the group can be considered under different headings: relevant or irrelevant, taught or not yet taught.

Relevant questions covering material which has already been taught should be answered by explaining the material again, preferably in a slightly different way, as it is clear that your earlier teaching did not get through to the student.

Relevant questions covering material which has not been taught may be answered briefly (if there is time and the answer will not serve to confuse or distract the student or the group.)

Alternatively, delay the question by explaining that it will be covered later, asking the student to remind you if it doesn't become clear.

Irrelevant questions serve as a distraction to the group and must be disposed of as quickly as possible. A student who persists in asking such questions is probably doing so to draw attention to himself. A quiet word away from the group to explain the effect he is having should be enough. If not, you will have to dispose of the questions firmly in front of the group. You will have their sympathy.

Teaching adults

Adults tend to have a greater fear of failure than children. They are therefore more reluctant to appear foolish in front of a class. You should concentrate on rewarding ideas and not on making those who give wrong answers feel inadequate. The 'Jenny was absolutely right when she said....but....' form of response is always helpful.

Adults who have always been lectured in an educational environment are initially reluctant to become involved in discussion, question and answer tests and quizzes etc. They expect the lecturer to talk continuously and dislike having to contribute themselves.

You will have to push against this dislike at first; once the students have overcome it they will learn more quickly and enjoy themselves more. Don't give anyone the opportunity to opt out. To encourage others, congratulate those who join in initially.

The greater part of adult learning since leaving centre will have been by problem solving and personal experience. Use this to your advantage and let reasoning from information you supply be one of your teaching methods, but remember that this approach usually takes longer than instruction.

An adult's academic interest in the subject is not always compatible with his practical ability; the gap sometimes widens with age.

Preparation and use of visual aids

Analysis of sources of information to the brain shows that sight plays a proportionately greater part in the learning process than all the other senses. Sight accounts for about 75% of input, hearing for about 15% and the other senses share the remaining 10%. a picture may not be worth exactly 1000 words but this analysis shows why the use of visual aids is so important - and why the avoidance of visual distractions is necessary.

Visual aids are usually used either to help or explain difficult concepts or to build up complicated ideas or techniques. They may also be used to emphasise or reinforce certain key points in your teaching.

Basic principles

Relevance – Visual aids should not be produced for their own sake. They must be relevant or they become a distraction.

Clarity – Diagrams must be easily understood and not contain irrelevant detail. They must be readable by the furthest of your audience. Any visual aid which cannot be seen clearly by everyone is neither visual nor an aid.

Timing – Don't produce visual aids until they are needed; they will only distract your audience if displayed too soon. Dispose of them after use.

Display – Try to display a visual aid in a dramatic manner. Students will remember something far longer if it is linked to a highlight.

Involvement – A display of neatly tied knots on a board is much less effective than students attempting to tie the knots themselves, although the knotboard will be useful for reference **after** the lesson.

Use the other senses. An aid which does something and which can be passed around is more valuable than something which is merely displayed. Beware of moving on to another topic while your visual aid is still circulating. Nobody will listen to you if they have a toy with which to play. Equally, use the mechanism of some visual aids to 'punctuate' your lecture and put in 'paragraphs' eg. switching off the OHP between acetates, lights on/off between slides.

Yourself – Don't forget that you are a walking visual aid with optional sound. Think about your mannerisms, delivery position etc. and their effect on the class. Never hide behind another visual aid so that your audience cannot see you properly. Finally, dress for the occasion. Although sailing is a practical sport, don't let your appearance serve as a distraction to your audience. A good general rule is to dress about as well as the best dressed of your audience - that way nobody will be offended.

TYPES OF VISUAL AID

Blackboard or whiteboard

Once the mainstay of the classroom teacher, the blackboard has certain advantages; it is readily available, does not require power, can be used continuously and can be seen by large numbers.

The disadvantages are that although adequate for simple messages or drawings it is unsatisfactory for doing detailed work when the audience is present. The information cannot be stored, successful use depends on a practised style and it is impossible to talk to your audience effectively while writing on the board.

The more recent alternative of the whiteboard has the advantage of being less messy to use but has all the other drawbacks of the blackboard.

Flipchart

Popular for business conferences, the flipchart has many of the characteristics of the blackboard but it is portable and information can be prepared in advance, stored and used repeatedly.

Powerpoint

Increasingly, Powerpoint has become the audio-visual aid of choice for shorebased instructors because of it's versatility and ease of use. There are some pitfalls however - beware of producing slides with too many distracting effects, animations and avoid colour clashes with background and text. Most instructors find it best to use simple diagrams, pictures and bulleted text, using Powerpoint as a prompt for teaching, rather than reading verbatim from slides.

Overhead projector

OHPs can be used in daylight without the instructor losing eye contact with the audience. Although it is possible to write or draw as you speak, most instructors prefer to prepare OHP acetates in advance. You can enhance them by use of colour and by using overlays to build up or break down complex concepts or techniques.

Once a few operating tricks are learnt the OHP is simple to use effectively but you must avoid the temptation to put too many words on an acetate. Remember that words are not visuals, even though they may be used to trigger thoughts or retain ideas.

Position the OHP so that it can be seen by all the class and eliminate the keystone effect by tilting the screen. Remember not to talk to the screen or to stand in front of it. Ensure that your acetates are in the correct sequence and rehearse any special effects such as masking or overlays.

Video/film

There are a number of professionally made videos available for shorebased courses, including some made by the RYA. You should ensure that you are familiar with the video before you show it. Videos and films are a good introduction and summary and can provide a 'change of voice', but they are most effective if shown in sections, with back-up teaching in between. Involve the class for feedback.

Models

Ranging from simple shapes used for collision avoidance talks to detailed models of yachts, the scope is limited only by the ability of the builder.

In general, a model should have only as much detail as is essential. Over-complication may be satisfying to the creator but can detract from its use as a visual aid.

APPENDIX 1

TYPICAL PRACTICAL COURSE BRIEFING

Sunday evening

1700	Victuals available for collection
1800	Students arrive
1900	Dinner - hire oilskins (if required)
2000	Briefing on board to include:

COURSE

1. Aims
2. Programme
3. Details of students' experience - swimmers?
4. Importance of clothing and boots
5. Seasickness

SAFETY

1. Lifejackets
2. Harnesses and Jackstay
3. Gas routine (put kettle on)
4. Fire extinguishers and blanket
5. Flares
6. Liferaft

HUSBANDRY

1. Explain menu
2. Cooking roster
3. Kitty and float
4. Gear stowage and tidiness
5. Heads and seacocks

YACHT

1. Basic layout below
2. Fresh water
3. Electrics
4. Engine operation

Monday morning

1. Stow gear ready for sea
2. Engine checks
3. Simple rigging. Deck layout
4. Bend on headsail

0900   Depart

TEACHING IDEAS FOR PRACTICAL INSTRUCTORS

Sailing exercises and techniques

Man overboard

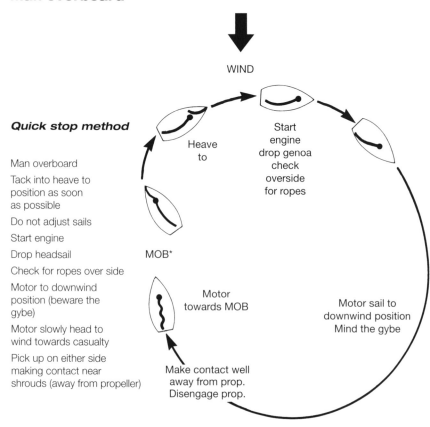

WIND

Quick stop method

Man overboard

Tack into heave to position as soon as possible

Do not adjust sails

Start engine

Drop headsail

Check for ropes over side

Motor to downwind position (beware the gybe)

Motor slowly head to wind towards casualty

Pick up on either side making contact near shrouds (away from propeller)

Heave to

Start engine drop genoa check overside for ropes

MOB*

Motor towards MOB

Motor sail to downwind position Mind the gybe

Make contact well away from prop. Disengage prop.

Sailing without a rudder

Lash the helm amidships and steer using the sails alone. Try to tack and gybe.

Mooring

One tack one gybe

Approach a wind with tide mooring on a close reach. From a position close to the buoy you are allowed one tack followed by one gybe to return to the buoy. It is best to demonstrate first.

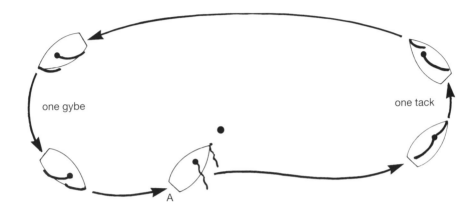

The exercise can be repeated but with the gybe first followed by the tack.

The importance of this exercise is identifying the approach position (A) which will result in the yacht close reaching to the buoy. It requires quick thinking and orientation. It can then be repeated on the other tack. Suitable for Coastal Skipper and above. If the mooring is not actually picked up it is a quick and intensive boat handling session.

Power exercises

Turning in own length. Use of prop kick. Steering astern.

Ferry gliding - using tide and gentle engine control to drift sideways.

Springing off.

Alongside astern.

Fore and aft moorings.

Motoring around a buoy in a strong tide keeping the yacht head to tide.

COASTAL SKIPPER/YACHTMASTER OFFSHORE EXAMINATION CHECK LIST

Prior to going to sea

Preparation of boat and crew

Safety brief

Stowage on deck/below

Boat checks

Engine checks

Crew brief

Watchkeeping plan

Sail selection

Passage planning

Selection of destination

Tidal calculations

Tidal stream prediction

Selection of charts (correction)

Selection of route - entering Waypoints

Prediction of CTS and ETA

Entering/leaving harbour

Boat handling

General		Use of warps
		Boat control under sail
		Boat control under power
		Briefing and use of crew
Specific	Berthing.	Alongside
Any 2 from		Piles
this list.		Buoy under sail
		Buoy under power
		Anchor under sail
		Anchor under power
	Unberthing.	Alongside
		Piles
		Buoy under sail
		Buoy under power
		Anchor under sail
		Anchor under power

Pilotage

Pilotage plan

Crew briefing and organisation

Control of boat

Execution of plan

At sea
Seamanship and boat handling

Helmsmanship

Sail trim

Sail selection

Man overboard recovery

Navigation and Chartwork

Position fixing – visual

Position fixing – RNAs

Use of GPS

Use of echo sounder

Course shaping

Working up EP

Keeping the log

Navigation in restricted visibility

Knowledge of: Buoyage

                     Chart symbols

Navigational strategy

Deck work and general seamanship

Safety of crew - use of harnesses

Sail changing

Chafe prevention

Lookout

Crew motivation and leadership

Preparations for heavy weather

Conduct in restricted visibility

Periodic engine checks

Specific subjects
IPRCS

Theoretical knowledge

Practical application

Meteorology

Knowledge of forecasts available

Interpretation and application of forecasts

Characteristics of highs and lows

Use of barometer and visual signs

APPENDIX 4

REPORTING SERIOUS ACCIDENTS

A report of any serious accident must be sent to the MAIB. within 24 hours.

A serious accident is:

1. A fatality.
2. A serious injury/illness requiring evacuation and/or hospitalisation. Loss of consciousness.
3. Loss or abandonment of yacht.
4. Serious disabling of the yacht, requiring her to be taken out of service for more than 24 hours.

INFORMATION NEEDED IN REPORTS

Reports should include the following:

Name of vessel, Code of Practice number.

Name and address of centre and owner.

Where bound to and from.

Name and port of registry or flag of any other vessel involved.

Sequence of events leading up to the incident.

Brief details of the incident:

Type (eg collision, fire, man overboard, serious injury).

Date, time, position of vessel.

Weather conditions.

Outcome of incident:

Number of persons killed or injured with brief details (names not necessary).

Extent of damage

Whether the incident caused pollution or hazard to navigation.

Conclusions of on-board investigations:

Cause

How a future similar accident might be avoided.

What action has been taken or recommended.

The report should be signed by the skipper or Principal and sent to:

Marine Accident Investigations Branch

5/7 Brunswick Place, Southampton, Hampshire SO15 2AN

Tel: Office hours   023 8039 5500

All hours   023 8023 2527

Fax   023 8023 2459

e-mail: maib@detr.gsi.gar.uk

RYA *Membership*

Promoting and Protecting Boating
www.rya.org.uk

RYA Membership

Promoting and Protecting Boating

The RYA is the national organisation which represents the interests of everyone who goes boating for pleasure.

The greater the membership, the louder our voice when it comes to protecting members' interests.

Apply for membership today, and support the RYA, to help the RYA support you.

Benefits of Membership

- Access to expert advice on all aspects of boating from legal wrangles to training matters
- Special members' discounts on a range of products and services including boat insurance, books, videos and class certificates
- Free issue of certificates of competence, increasingly asked for by everyone from overseas governments to holiday companies, insurance underwriters to boat hirers

- Access to the wide range of RYA publications, including the quarterly magazine
- Third Party insurance for windsurfing members
- Free Internet access with RYA-Online
- Special discounts on AA membership
- Regular offers in RYA Magazine
- ...and much more

Join now - membership form opposite

Join online at *www.rya.org.uk*

Visit our website for information, advice, members' services and web shop.

① **Important** To help us comply with Data Protection legislation, please tick *either* Box A or Box B (you must tick Box A to ensure you receive the full benefits of RYA membership). The RYA will not pass your data to third parties.

☐ A. I wish to join the RYA and receive future information on member services, benefits (as listed in RYA Magazine and website) and offers.

☐ B. I wish to join the RYA but do not wish to receive future information on member services, benefits (as listed in RYA Magazine and website) and offers.

When completed, please send this form to: RYA, RYA House, Ensign Way, Hamble, Southampton, SO31 4YA

②

Title	Forename	Surname	Date of Birth (DD / MM / YY)	Male	Female
1.			/ /	☐	☐
2.			/ /	☐	☐
3.			/ /	☐	☐
4.			/ /	☐	☐

Address

Town   County   Post Code

Evening Telephone   Daytime Telephone

email

...nature: Date:

③ **Type of membership required:** *(Tick Box)*

☐ *Personal* Annual rate £39 or £36 by Direct Debit

☐ *Under 21* Annual rate £13 (no reduction for Direct Debit)

☐ *Family** Annual rate £58 or £55 by Direct Debit

* Family Membership: 2 adults plus any under 21s all living at the same address

Please see Direct Debit form overleaf

④ Please tick ONE box to show your main boating interest.

☐ Yacht Racing   ☐ Yacht Cruising
☐ Dinghy Racing   ☐ Dinghy Cruising
☐ Personal Watercraft   ☐ Inland Waterways
☐ Powerboat Racing   ☐ Windsurfing
☐ Motor Boating   ☐ Sportsboats and RIBs

Instructions to your Bank or Building Society to pay by Direct Debit

Please complete this form and return it to:
Royal Yachting Association, RYA House, Ensign Way, Hamble, Southampton, Hampshire SO31 4YA

Originators Identification Number

9	5	5	2	1	3

To The Manager: Bank/Building Society

Address:

Post Code:

2. Name(s) of account holder(s)

3. Branch Sort Code

4. Bank or Building Society account number

Banks and Building Societies may not accept Direct Debit instructions for some types of account

Cash, Cheque, Postal Order enclosed £
Made payable to the Royal Yachting Association

077 | Office use only: Membership Number Allocated

5. RYA Membership Number (For office use only)

6. Instruction to pay your Bank or Building Society

Please pay Royal Yachting Association Direct Debits from the account detailed in this instruction subject to the safeguards assured by The Direct Debit Guarantee.
I understand that this instruction may remain with the Royal Yachting Association and, if so, details will be passed electronically to my Bank/Building Society.

Signature(s)

Date

Office use / Centre Stamp